SOCIALISM IS A MORAL IDEA

SOCIALISM IS A MORAL IDEA. IT'S SAYING EVERYONE'S IMPORTANT AND THE ECONOMY MUST BE ORGANISED TO INCLUDE EVERYBODY. GORBACHEV SAID, 'PEASANTS HAVE ALWAYS TAKEN TOMATOES TO MARKET,' MEANING MARKETS ARE NOT ALL EVIL. BUT MONOPOLIES ARE EVIL AND DISTORTED POWER AND GREAT INEQUALITY IS EVIL.

First published in 2019 by Martin Firrell Company Ltd.
10 Queen Street Place, London EC4R 1AG, United Kingdom.

ISBN 978-1-912622-07-8

Devised and edited by Martin Firrell.

© Copyright Martin Firrell Company 2019.

All rights reserved. No part of this publication may be reproduced, stored in or introduced into a retrieval system, or transmitted, in any form, or by any means (electronic, mechanical, photocopying, recording or otherwise) without the prior written consent of the publisher.

This book is sold subject to the condition that it shall not, by way of trade or otherwise, be lent, re-sold, hired out, or otherwise circulated without the publisher's prior consent in any form of binding or cover other than that in which it is published and without a similar condition including this condition being imposed on the subsequent purchaser.

Text is set in Baskerville, 11pt on 17pt.

Baskerville is a serif typeface designed in 1754 by John Baskerville (1706-1775) in Birmingham, England. Compared to earlier typeface designs, Baskerville increased the contrast between thick and thin strokes. Serifs were made sharper and more tapered, and the axis of rounded letters was placed in a more vertical position. The curved strokes were made more circular in shape, and the characters became more regular.

Baskerville is categorised as a transitional typeface between classical typefaces and high contrast modern faces. Of his own typeface, John Baskerville wrote, 'Having been an early admirer of the beauty of letters, I became insensibly desirous of contributing to the perfection of them. I formed to myself ideas of greater accuracy than had yet appeared, and had endeavoured to produce a set of types according to what I conceived to be their true proportion.'

CLARE SHORT

Clare Short was born in Birmingham on 15 February 1946. Her mother's family had lived in Handsworth for two generations but originally came from County Clare. Her father came from Crossmaglen in County Armagh, Northern Ireland. She was educated at St. Paul's Grammar School, Birmingham and at the Universities of Keele and Leeds where she studied Political Science, graduating BA (Hons).

Clare was elected to Parliament in 1983 as MP for her home constituency of Birmingham Ladywood. During the years of Labour's opposition, she served as Shadow Minister for Women (1993-1995), Shadow Secretary of State for Transport (1995-1996) and Opposition Spokesperson for Overseas Development (1996-1997). She was a member of Labour's National Executive Committee (NEC) from 1988-1997 and Chair of the NEC's Women's Committee (1993-1996).

When Labour came to power in 1997, Clare was appointed Secretary of State for International Development, elevating the previous Overseas Development Agency into a full government department. She oversaw the transformation of the previous agency into the newly independent Department for International Development (DfID). Clare resigned from the Government in 2003 in opposition to the Iraq War. As a backbench MP, she continued to advocate development causes and hold the Government to account on issues affecting her constituents. In 2006 she resigned the Labour whip in protest against the conduct of the Blair government. She became an Independent Labour Party Member of Parliament and used this position to campaign against Britain's democratic deficit and in favour of proportional representation.

TRANSCRIPT

Clare Short, Secretary of State for International Development (1997-2003), in conversation with public artist Martin Firrell, 14 May 2018.

— Martin Firrell: **What's your first memory of understanding that power was present in the world?**

— **Clare Short:** I'm not sure this is a complete answer to your question but I'm one of seven children and when I was little my dad used to take us for walks at Christmas (kids get so excited they become ridiculous and you have to do something with them). I must have been four or five, or something like that. You know those boxes, usually outside newsagents, that had postcards with adverts on them? He pointed one of them out and it said, 'Room to let. No Irish or coloureds.' I saw more like that later, but I remember that one clearly. My father was Irish and these were the very beginnings of migration from the Caribbean; the Indian subcontinent came a bit later. It wasn't exactly an expression of power: if you have a room to let, you're not exactly rich. But excluding people like that is a wrong that you need to do something about. I suppose that story's about the absence of power or needing to get some power to change the injustice. It's just that I remember that very strongly and I was really very small.

— **When were you aware that some people had power and some people didn't?**

— I grew up in this household where my father was a very political person. Not in the sense of aspiring to political office but in the way he looked at the world. He was certainly very interested in Irish history and very cross that, when Ireland eventually became free, it was partitioned and his village was just north of the border.[1] He was a teacher. And he gave us the sense that the British Empire was a bad, oppressive thing. He didn't give us lectures. It wasn't like that. It was just the ambience. For example, I was ten when the Suez crisis was on and British troops were mobilised in 1956.[2] In my class at school - it's another of those deep memories from my childhood, it was quite a poor area, Handsworth, a Catholic school, forty odd kids in a class - the children all started singing, 'We'll throw Nasser in the Suez Canal.' And I got them all together and said, 'This isn't right. It's their canal. They are allowed to take over the canal. It belongs to the Egyptians.' You see I'm trying to answer your question truthfully. I think it was a sort of perspective on life and the world. But equally, my father would go rushing off when some children from his school, maybe at the weekend, were evicted from the room they were in. That was the era of Rachman and very horrible landlordism.[3] So the sense that things were unfair - both internationally and at home - and that we had to resist that unfairness was in my understanding of the world from childhood. Power existed and it was not being used properly. There was the sense that we have to do something to get that to change. And because of the mood of the times, there was the sense that change was possible too.

— **Did those experiences lead you directly to seek power, to be able to do something? Was that the beginning of the desire for political power or did that come much later?**

— That came later. I'm saying this in answer to your question about the sense that there is power and it needs to be used to change things, but I think mine was a collective sense that 'we' needed to act.

When I was at school I thought I'd be a teacher. There are teachers on both sides of my family, lots of them, plus the odd priest and a few nuns. I have lots of cousins. Then I found out that people like us could go to university. In those days it was only six or seven percent of the population, so people like us didn't used to go. My dad used to talk about 'university people' with a sort of reverence. He was what Gramsci called 'an organic intellectual'.[4] He naturally read and thought in that kind of way. It was so exciting and I thought, 'I'll go to university.' I wanted to know more and understand the world. I wanted to do political science and some economics and some political philosophy. I wanted to know what was right, and how we know what's right. How we can make the economy work differently. Sociology was a big subject then and I loved it all. I wasn't for a minute thinking, 'I'm going to be a politician.' I was just trying to understand it all. I did a course on Black Power and the Civil Rights Movement.[5] So this was about '65? I graduated in '68. I was just watching and looking and trying to understand all these things going on in the world and I was excited by it. Then I thought I would take the exams to go into the Civil Service. There used to be a very elitist entry system for the Civil Service. The appeal for me was really to go and see the British establishment at work, just to understand it. And you have to get a job. So I did. I went to the Home Office. That's when I became a private secretary to a succession of Ministers. I was there through an election, and I worked for Mark Carlisle[6] in the election, then Alex Lyon[7]. You organise their office for them and give them their papers and tell them where they've got to be tomorrow. When they go to the House of Commons, you go over with the appropriate officials to make sure they get the briefing on what they need etc. And it was really when I saw all those MPs that it went 'click' in my mind, 'Good heavens, I could be one of those.' Prior to that, it never even crossed my mind that someone like me could be a Member of Parliament. I think by then I'd been a member of the Labour Party since 1970 in Leeds and worked in the election and cared about changing the Government. It was when Wilson lost and we thought we were going to win and boot Keith Josephs out. That was the seat we were working in. But my moment on the road to Damascus was seeing those MPs. And I think this is really important as a general perception. Nowadays people talk about mentoring. I never had any mentors but somehow people have to see those in power to understand that they are normal, feeble humans like everybody else. This was when I thought, 'I don't want to be in the Civil Service all the time.' I wasn't at all biased because I understand my biases unlike a lot of people. I was a good private secretary to a Conservative Minister. I argued with him once because some Tory MP had written in saying there was someone in his constituency who was agitating in a trade union calling for a strike, and could they get any background on him. And my minister said, 'Can we get any background on this?' And I said, 'You shouldn't do this. Haven't you read John Stuart Mill? This isn't right.' I think he put the note in and he passed it onto the department and then he came back and said, 'You were quite right. I've got another way of doing it.' But I loved policy and how you make the prisons better and the police more responsive - these were all the things we had in the Home Office. We had Northern Ireland just up some backstairs and so on. We had the Ugandan Asian Crisis[8] when I was there so I cared about all that and loved it but I didn't want to be neutral. When I saw these MPs and, I suppose, Ministers, I thought, 'That's it! I can go there and put these things right by speaking out clearly for what I believe in.' That was my light on the road to Damascus.

— **Can I ask you a question about a couple of things you said? First of all you said, 'People like us don't go to university' and then you said, 'People like me didn't become politicians.' What do those two things mean?**

— Well, I mean it's sociologically the case. I wasn't feeling deprived. I grew up in this kind of stroppy, happy family where I think we all felt quite good about ourselves. But we weren't posh or rich or anything like that. We were proud of our father being a teacher and a headteacher. My grandad - my mother's father - was a tool maker at Lucas's[9] which is a very skilled working-class job. So I never had a sense that people like us are inferior or no good or have to be humble. In those days I wanted to be a teacher and I thought I'd go to teacher training college. I suppose no one told me to do it but I liked the idea and I respected teachers. I still do. And the profession is being destroyed. And if you look sociologically, this was the expansion of the new universities.

Nowadays fifty percent of the population go to university but then it was a very exclusive, very small social group that went. It only expanded to seven percent of the age cohort in my time. So you understand I was really proud of 'persons like us' but I also knew there was a rich, posh, not-fair group that ran a lot of things, and that we weren't part of them. What was the other thing I said? 'People like us didn't become MPs.' Well, indeed. Yes, is being a girl in there? I'm one of five sisters and two brothers. My dad was working, my mum was at home and there was the classic thing of his being at meetings and coming home late while mum held the fort. But we were all made to do our share of the washing up and making beds. When my brothers left home and went to university, there were all these women saying, 'Stop oppressing us,' (because this was the height of Seventies feminism) and they were saying, 'What? I've grown up with these stroppy sisters telling me what to do.' I never felt weak because I was a girl. I felt comfortable in my own skin. It was more 'people like us' than 'me, girl', I think.

— **Presumably, as you started working as an adult, at some point you encountered some sense of, 'make the tea, dear.'**

— Yes. I went to the Home Office in 1970 and I was absolutely clear that I wasn't going to learn to type. There was the clerical class, the executive class, and the administrative class, and I was an entry into the administrative class. There were some who had come into the executive class and been promoted and were in relatively senior positions although they didn't go right to the top. And some of them would type their own memos and things. They were men, the ones I'm thinking of now. But I saw it as a trap for a girl to learn to type. 'I'm not doing that. I know where that might lead me.' I was very clear about that.

— And very ambitious by the sounds of it in that you had your sights set on where that might lead and how that might become a trap, holding you back.

— Except I remember one of my contemporaries saying, 'Why don't you stay in the Civil Service and become Dame Clare Short.' And I didn't want that. So I wasn't ambitious.

— Did he know you? Had he met you?

— Well, no. He was quite an ironic person as well. So I could have. I mean it was then a very clear structure and if you were reasonably bright and worked hard, you could. It's a very kind of fair, well… it's very Oxbridge, but there's open promotion systems in it but that didn't draw me, so… ambition…? I think it was more that I was greedy to do things rather than having a calculating ambition. That's true of my whole political career, actually. I never did calculate where I was going. So it wasn't quite ambition. It was kind of, 'I want to get things done. I want to change things. And I want to be in there in the thick of it.'

— **And was part of that wanting to change things about social justice?**

— Absolutely. Absolutely. That just came with my Weetabix. I can remember going to a gala of Birmingham schools with my dad and his school had scruffy swimming costumes unlike the schools with splendid black costumes. And there was one little girl who was ever such a slow swimmer and she came in last. Why do I remember that so graphically? It's this sense that things aren't fair and things have got to change. In the street I grew up in, there were some sisters who were all very plump and one tried to commit suicide. All of us children went and looked at the pavement and we were sure we saw drops of blood. I'm sure we didn't really. And when she came back they prosecuted her, you know they used to.[10] Things like that. I still feel furious about that. I didn't really know her. She was a good deal older than us but I knew her by sight. She was so in despair that she tried to take her own life and the fact that she survived meant that she had committed a criminal offence and she could be prosecuted.

I also remember going to other children's houses - you

know for birthday parties and that kind of thing - and seeing people with much less. We didn't have a posh house but some of the other houses were very poor. We were warm and had good blankets (we all just had one fire in the living room then, no central heating, nobody had it) but there were girls in my class at school who wore pumps with holes in them and cotton clothes in the winter when it was really cold. I can still remember. So this concern for social justice wasn't just theoretical. I knew things weren't fair and could be better.

— **Can I ask you about the route from saying, 'I could be an MP.' What was the actual route to getting there?**

— There used to be a Labour Party branch that met in my parents' house to organise things like delivering leaflets at election times. I was fourteen or fifteen at the time, so I knew that structure. I think my dad fell in and out of the Labour Party at different times because of its policy on Ireland. I joined. I didn't do so much in student politics at Leeds. I joined the local Labour Party. So that says something - that I was choosing that more rooted activism, and I worked in that election in 1970. I knew that once you're active in the Labour Party then there's a route to putting yourself forward for selection. I was living in Battersea at the time and I was in the Battersea Labour Party. I was quite active and campaigning, knocking on doors and putting out leaflets and all the rest. And being at meetings and arguing over policy. There was a system then. I don't know if it even still exists. There were B lists of people that the local party thought could be considered as a possible candidate. Battersea did things very openly and they were looking to nominate people to that list and I was asked if I wanted to be considered. Saying I wanted to be nominated was the most embarrassing thing in the whole of my political life. I found it intensely embarrassing to put myself forward in that way. But I did and then they interviewed all the people. There were about ten people on the committee and they all voted that I should go forward which I felt wonderful about. So declaring my ambition - declaring that I thought I could be considered - was excruciatingly embarrassing.

— **Why?**

— I don't know, but it was.

— **How old were you then, when you were declaring?**

— How old was I then? About thirty.

— **So you weren't a youngster?**

— I wasn't a spring chicken, no. I can still feel the embarrassment when I talk about it. It's just that it's so proud and arrogant and it's on the edge of that self-seeking. It's one of the reasons why I don't like all of that leadership culture, today, where everyone has to be very thrusting and put themselves forward. I like systems that pick up people of talent and nurture them and say, 'What about you?' This is a broader point. I'm not just talking about myself. I think people who push themselves forward are not always the ones with all the talent. We need systems that include others who somehow don't feel entitled to be pushy but have got lots of valuable qualities. This culture of stress on leadership came about in the last fifteen or twenty years, I think, when they ran these endless leadership courses. They used to ask me to speak at them sometimes and I'd say, 'I want to know who's running the followership course!'

I'm not saying it was right that I felt embarrassed but I did. Maybe it was because of class, sex, gender that it seemed I wasn't the kind of person that should be wanting that, I don't know. But I put myself forward and then people started inviting me to go to selections. I went to a couple but my little dream was to represent my area. Then that came up. There was a woman, who we knew, who was the MP, and was standing down. I went to be considered and I didn't get it the first time round. And then I was selected. Then there was a merger of the two constituencies. I think there would have been far more former MPs trying to get it but they knew there was going to be a merger of two constituencies so if they got chosen in the first place they might lose it again. I got selected and then selected again when the two constituencies were put together. Basically Sir Albert Bore,[11] as he now is, was the alternative candidate and he was a big lefty at the time. So the left split and the right came to me, I got them! So there I was. Once I was in the system, I was happy to go for it and try. But it's a good question. There must be loads of people who've got no idea how you'd approach it. I used to get letters from people saying, 'I'd like to be an MP. How do you do it?' And I used to write back and say, 'You have to decide which party you support and then go and be an activist and join in and do some work, participate in meetings and learn to speak up, maybe even organise, take on an office.' People sort of thought, 'I can fly in out of the blue.' Perhaps more people can do that these days. It was certainly true in Blair's time. If there were journalists he liked or people he liked, he'd then fix seats for them but that's only when all the power is stacked in one way and someone has got the patronage. If you are not in those kinds of systems or don't approve of them, there was this quite fair system that you could apply to. That's what I did. Many are called and few are chosen.

— **In that journey did you feel that you encountered challenges because you were a woman?**

— I didn't, honestly. I think I saw it as luck and politics. Gender wasn't in my mind. I got a shock when I got to the Commons. There are 650 MPs and only about 30 women on both sides together. When the house is full that's a tiny number. Some of the older women - the Thatcher generation and Joan Maynard[12] on our side - used to talk about steel and taxes and not nurseries because they had to prove they were as good as the men. Whereas my generation thought we could talk about steel and taxes and nurseries and cervical cancer and whatever, which was probably a reflection of Seventies feminism in us. We were more confident that this was our agenda and we were entitled to it. And of course, by then I was older. The whole question of sexual oppression - men pinching your bottom and all that kind of stuff, which used to go on widely - I became more and more sensitive to that whole agenda and all the women who lost out and had to do all the childcare and had low incomes, so it just became part of my life in a very natural way. I wasn't in a woman's group, for example, in the Seventies and it was women in that era who, outside the formal system, built up the hostels for battered women so they had somewhere to run to. I always admired that enormously. You know, I had my son and he was adopted and I always admired lone parent women who'd made it, who'd managed even with great difficulty. So it was life that made me broaden my agenda. I started off with quite a deeply political agenda that was about inequality in Britain and internationally. I was a stroppy little girl. I assumed that girls could do what boys could do or as good as. And it was when I was older and sex and all that rears its head and you see the patterns. And I just took it all in and felt an obligation to speak up for it.

— **Can we talk about power now? Because, in a way, of all the women I'm speaking to, you are the one woman who had real elected representative power. You were there to use the power given to you by the voters to do stuff. So you actually definitely had power in your hands didn't you - or did you?**

— It was Aneurin Bevan[13] - a coal miner originally - who said something like, 'I wanted some power to change things so I went on the local council and it wasn't there, so I went to the county council and I went to Parliament and I went to the Cabinet…' Something like that, and I think you're quite right, as a local MP, you've got some power but in the face of Parliament and the Government you don't feel very powerful. I did feel very, very strongly that I had authority to approach the system and demand that something was changed for individuals, and that authority resided in me because the people had given me their votes. It was my duty to be available to them so they could come to me and I could say, 'This isn't right.' I did that. I used to sit and hundreds and hundreds of people used to come to see me. Very frequently the system wasn't giving them what they were entitled to, let alone the unfairnesses in the system. And I felt that very strongly. So that's a kind of power and I'm still living in my old constituency half the time and people still come up to me and say, 'Oh, you sorted out my house,' or 'You sorted out my granny's something...' That's the bread and butter work. Some MPs used to say, 'I don't want to be a social worker.' But I think that's the wrong attitude. Also, when all those people are coming to see you and you see the patterns of where things are hurting and how those patterns change, you learn from them. That's the day-to-day life of the people who vote for you and you're both helping them out and being accessible to them and you're learning what hurts them. There's a bias in it - I thought about this afterwards - towards people who have got more needs, but then there are all sorts of meetings in the constituency and people come and tell you what they think. So that is a form of power but it's a limited power. Then there's the question of how do you change what's causing these problems? And if you're in opposition, the power you have is to voice it, to just speak up and say, 'This is wrong.' You can do that in the Commons. But then, if you're going to challenge the system, you have to be in the power structures of your party. Otherwise you're just a voice. Otherwise you're just available to people and available to speak up for the things they care about, which is not nothing, but it's a very limited power. There's something about speaking the truth even when you can't win that's important. I think it's been forgotten. People really care about it even if you didn't succeed. People care that someone was saying those things. I still believe in that. In the Thatcher years it was especially true. We saw a massive increase in unemployment in my area. Lots of people lost their jobs and we had riots and all sorts of things that had never happened before. And at least we could speak up about that truth. So that's the first aspect of power. Then if you want your party to win and you want to help to shape how your party behaves, you have to climb the slippery slope of your own party.

Now I have to say, soon after I got to the Commons, I was invited to be on the front bench team, I think it was John Prescott, unemployment. I'd only been there a short time but I had been working for the Unemployment Unit and Youthaid. I did know things about youth unemployment and the structural problems of unemployment. That opportunity came very quickly and I wasn't really seeking it. I think John Prescott went to the library and there were things people had written and I'd spoken a little bit. So I found that getting on the front bench, it just came out of the blue, very immediately. People don't realise when they say, 'Shadow Minister for this and that', there's something like a hundred people in government, in the Cabinet, junior Ministers and whips. You have about three hundred when you're in power so the chances of being promoted are pretty high - one in three. It's what makes everyone so craven actually. So in opposition, you have the same numbers, because you have to oppose of all that. Then there's the National Executive which used to be more powerful. Blair diminished it. I think it might be becoming more powerful again. It lays down policy and structure and constitutional change. There were some seats for women dating back to the early days of the Labour Party, and the suffrage movement. There were trade union elected seats, constituency party elected seats, and there were these women's seats, of which I think there were five, and they were voted on by both the constituency party and the trade unions. I was sponsored by NUPE, a wonderful, lovely union of low paid public sector workers. It merged into UNISON later. Rodney Bickerstaffe,[14] who died recently, was the General Secretary and there were lots of dinner ladies and cleaners, and it was the most cuddly lovely union you could imagine. I was sponsored by them and obviously it was mostly women, overwhelmingly. So they voted for me. Again you see it was me, it was the hardest thing to declare that I wanted to be an MP. I got elected onto the National Executive and that was '87. I was on it for ten years and we were doing all the reforms to try and make ourselves capable of winning. These were the Neil Kinnock years and then the John Smith years, and massive reform took place. There's a sort of false story that everything was crazy until New Labour came along. That's not true. I was very active working through all the policies and dealing with the Trotskyist infiltration problem, and that was real power actually. It's behind-the-scenes work and you don't necessarily get the credit for it, but I took all of that very seriously. Then, I was a front bench spokesperson. I resigned twice. I got invited back. People say if you're calculating about your political career you shouldn't resign. The first time I resigned was over the Prevention of Terrorism Act renewal.[15] Although Labour had always opposed it, I objected when Neil said, 'That's it. We've all got to vote against.' It wasn't that I disagreed, it's just that I don't take well to diktat. If you do vote against the party line then you can't be on the front bench. That's one of the rules. So people who want to rise tend to 'brown nose' as they say. One of the things I did on the NEC was to chair the Women's Committee. By then we'd had all sorts of efforts to have more women elected to Parliament - things like 'there must be one woman on the shortlist' - and it hadn't worked. So we looked at what the Scandinavians had done and they all had quota systems. Of course, if you have proportional systems with lists, it's very easy to say three men, three women or whatever. But with our single member constituencies it's more difficult. Of course this was pre- '97 so we knew we were going to take a lot of seats. It was an opportunity to bring more women into Parliament, to put right a historic wrong, and make the party more representative of its voters. So we paired winnable seats saying one of them had to have an all-women shortlist. Some men said that was unfair but I kept insisting, 'Look, it's a fifty-fifty chance and the point is you're not fixing which woman will be chosen. You can have a tall one, a short one, a leftwing one, a rightwing one, a nice one, a nasty one. You know, you have a choice but you'll get half women.' So we got the big increase. I was part of all that and that was what drove it, getting more women into the House of Commons. I was not the only player in that but a significant one. John Smith was a very significant player in supporting it against plenty of opposition. Then the logic of that flowed through to 'we should have a quota for elections to the Shadow Cabinet'. I stood for the Shadow Cabinet and I got elected on the quota just a year or two before we went into government. So I suppose I put myself forward in that instance and did want it and knew we were going into government and, in the constitution of the Labour Party, the leader is supposed to be obliged to make the last elected Shadow Cabinet, the Cabinet. But you see, my story is like, yes I work hard, yes I care about things and I'm serious but these kind of promotions came to me. I wasn't a wilting flower, I mean I was up for it, but I didn't have to trample on somebody else to get elected. Although I remember there was one, I think it was Renée Short[16] - she was a Wolverhampton MP, not any relation of mine - and she was on the National Executive and I was elected. Actually, I think she had fallen off before and I know she really was cross with me as though I'd trampled on her. But that's not true. So I know people can see it, but tides come and if you are the kind of person people want and you do the work, you go forward. Well, that's how it was for me.

— **That's really interesting because my perception of politics and power is that everyone is constantly conniving and seeing how they can find their way forward. It's quite aggressive and not necessarily the best people rise to the top, but the people who are most keen to rise to the top.**

— I think there are those people you've just described. I

think there are quite a lot of those. And of course, I think some of this comes down to one of the advantages of including women - that they are usually outsiders. But that won't last forever. Some of them may come from political families and their parents may have been MPs and Ministers and so on but as women they take a different stance. Whereas men, who've always been in the system, think they have to do what you've just described and they do do it. But there's a mix. I'm sure there are some people who just put themselves forward and get chosen and there are others who calculate and trample on their best friend.

— **Do you think there's a difference between the way women and men regard power in politics, in your experience?**

— I've just made the point about the outsiderness of women. Now I think it's forty percent of Labour MPs are women, is that right? It's something like that. It used to be less than ten percent in my time so it's changing what it is that women bring. If it's normal for women to be there, then they are no longer outsiders in the political system. They might be reflecting some of the inequalities in the wider society, but, I don't know, I'm intrigued by this. In all systems, political especially, but in any organisation recruiting people, you need to do more than simply replicate the group in charge, you need ways of drawing in people who aren't naturally of the 'in' group. You need different people of ability and there are plenty of them who bring fresh perspectives and different ideas. Women are symbolic of that but not the only people because there's class and ethnicity and so on. I'm very clear that women are not always nicer. Some are but then we had Mrs Thatcher. Whatever you think of her, she proves that women aren't always nicer and softer and kinder. I mean lots of people admire her for being very tough and hard and the changes she brought through. And I'm very clear that, in all structures, having roughly equal numbers of men and women improves everything. Not just the life chances of the women, that's important, but actually the quality of the organisation and the quality of the policy-making and interaction.

This links to my views on over-emphasising leadership. By drawing in people who have got knowledge and batting ideas around you get a better outcome than any one person could have come up with on their own. I did that in my time at the Department for International Development and it's a joy that kind of policy-making. If everyone writes and thinks and brings forward their papers, you'll end up with something that no one had thought of in the first place, but something better. It builds on the knowledge of different people. I love that. I think we've lost a lot of that kind of policy-making and thinking. I think there might be a bit of a turn taking place against the very hierarchical leader. I saw a thing in the paper today. People were complaining that the CEO of Shell gets seven million a year. I mean, please, its just ridiculous. It's wrong, but it's completely foolish. What does he do with it? He can't be that much better than the other people he's working with. I just don't believe it for a second in any way. I don't think you get a quality organisation by doing things like that. I'm digressing from women but I'm not really, because I'm a bit intrigued by this. Because women are outsiders and they come in, they improve things. As it becomes normal for women to be there, they won't be outsiders and we have to watch it because you can get some ambitious women with sharp elbows like the old-fashioned, ambitious men with sharp elbows and then, you're getting equal opportunities for sharp elbowed, ambitious people but you're not getting the inclusion of women as a transformative force. In the Seventies argument about feminism, it wasn't just, 'We women have been oppressed and we want to be included.' It was, 'We can have a better society if everyone is included and women can be both powerful and clever as well as important and kind and look after their children and their elderly parents. And men can be everything men are, and men aren't trapped into being macho, powerful. They can be soft and gentle and have time with their children and we can have a society where we can all be what we are and it will be kinder and more interesting and more fulfilling for everybody.' That was very much part of feminism and I still believe in that. So, if you see what I mean, including women should be carrying this whole agenda with it. It's become almost fashionable with every issue that's raised about women's equality to talk about a women's power agenda. It's quite a change and all the newspapers are there. But there's an alternative agenda - the transformative inclusion of women agenda - and I like the transformative one.

— **I read a piece that said having more women CEOs won't mean that capitalism is transformed into a kind and benevolent system. It'll be just as ruthless and as horrendous as ever but with women in charge instead of men. I think that's very interesting. There are two schools of thought aren't there? One is: nothing changes, just some women end up earning seven million pounds a year. Then there's the other school of thought which says: everything could change. In a lot of the things you've said, there's been a pattern. I think this is about socialism in the fullest sense of the word, about groups co-operating to make things better. Policy is**

better. Parliament can be better. Society can be better when people are allowed to interrelate and find each other and find what they have to contribute.

— This is also relevant to the argument about race. I think Obama made a speech early on asking the question, are we demanding the right to be equally unequal? You know, black people and women and gay people. Is that what it is? And I think for some it is that: 'Well, we've got a fair society, it's very unequal but there's equal numbers of women and black people and gay people.' For me that just won't do. Just walking down Oxford Street, I'm looking at all these people shopping and yet I read something this morning about the number of people in Britain who say that they have encountered high levels of stress and considered suicide. The statistics were very high, one in four…? And I'm thinking, there's something wrong. All these people shopping, all these things that people can buy and everyone on their phones etc and there's so much unhappiness and loneliness. So one part of my argument is about this transformation for fairness and inclusion but I also think we're losing something - humans interacting and liking each other and irritating each other and arguing about what to do and having some shared power, even if it's about the local swimming baths, that kind of thing. I think there's something good in that that makes human beings happy and makes them think about others and actually it's one of the ironies: altruism makes you happy and yet you can't be altruistic in order to make yourself happy. I think this is a profoundly important argument around race equality, gender equality and it's got lost a bit, this transformative possibility. Yet I think that people know we need some transformation. I sent a copy of an article from the FT to a friend in America. The article claimed that most people say capitalism is a bad thing in America, the word 'capitalism'. I'm not dreaming of some kind of Soviet style revolution, of course not. I've never been attracted to that. I always knew I'd be in the Gulag if I was there, no question. And I used to think, some of those Tory MPs on the other side, they'd be quite happy in that kind of system. The question is this: capitalism, what are we going to do with it? Something's wrong. I think it might be heading for crisis. What happens if we get to the point where there aren't enough people with money to keep consuming? You know all the biggest companies are absolutely engorged with capital they can't spend. What happens when Apple and all of the richest companies in the world have all the money? Capitalism's got a crisis in its own structure. But then people even in America, ordinary folk, this article said, are saying they didn't like capitalism. But we haven't got anyone advocating a different system. Hard-nosed market neoliberalism has been so dominant for so long.[17] So what I'm really saying is, the thing that's leading to populism and nastiness is the kind of very hierarchical form of capitalism and its linked to this question we're discussing. Do you have inclusive systems of managing things? Leadership styles that are bringing out the best in everybody and getting everyone to the table? And I think we're either going to have a corrective or we're going to have a lot of nastiness and trouble. I know I've gone beyond the topic of gender but it is a really significant question. What is the inclusion of women meant to do? Are we demanding a right to be equally unequal or is it something more than that and for me, it's something more.

— Can I ask about socialism? What do you understand by socialism yourself? What it is for you, and the future?

— I think socialism is a moral idea. It's saying everyone's important and the economy must be organised to include everyone and care for everybody. Therefore socialists are drawn much more to public provision than private profit-seeking. Discussing how best to achieve this, people were drawn to monopolistic public ownership à la Soviet Union - very great concentrations of power and one party states (which were very common in newly independent countries in Africa, for example). But lots of abuse came with that, and inefficiencies. The result is abuse of power and inefficiency and getting rid of the vibrant creativity that you need to have a good society and innovation. The argument about how to do socialism was there from the beginning. The Soviet model was not the one that people advocated early on. There was an anarchistic trend where you just diffuse power and everybody does what they should do together. But in the course of my youth, I saw that socialism moved me and I saw it as a moral word. I became absolutely clear that the core of it is moral. So if the best way of organising the economy is to have the private sector having a significant role - a Keynesian[18] kind of mixed economy (which is what history and experience tells us) - then that's the more moral approach. The question is: how is everybody looked after? It is not about an ideological determination to have one model of economic organisation. Gorbachev said it when he was trying to change the Soviet Union. He had a good try poor old Gorbachev. He said, 'Peasants have always taken tomatoes to market.' You know, markets are not all evil. But most monopolies are evil and distorted power and great inequality is evil. 'What is socialism and why people are drawn to it?' I think this is an under-discussed question. It's probably less popular to say you are a socialist than to say you are a feminist at the moment. That might be changing with Corbyn, I don't know. But even that, I don't hear him keep saying, 'I'm a socialist.' He says things are unfair.

— The media use the term 'socialist' like it's a terrible criticism to be a socialist, or to be a committed socialist is a sort of political liability.

— It's a liability to be hardline, intolerant, ideological. Since Thatcher there's a big group both in America and here who just absolutely believe the market is the answer to everything. Always more market. Not looking at the consequences for people. It's just pure ideology. Like someone who would say the Soviet Union was a really good model and we should follow that example. There are probably not that many of those people left, but there are some. Socialism has become a word that's seen as unfashionable. But then we're in a muddle. I've just been reading, *How Will Capitalism End?* by a German author called Wolfgang Streeck. He's saying we all assume that there'll be a battle of ideologies, as there was in the past, and if capitalism fails, some kind of socialist model will come. He says that won't happen, it will all just end collapsing in on itself in a great big chaotic mess. I think that is the danger at the moment. There aren't many writers or big public figures who are describing a better society that people can say 'yes!' to. You don't get transformation until people feel something better is possible and practical, which is what happened in 1945. Nobody can talk about socialism now - it's as if it's too embarrassing. This is partly to do with Stalin and the Soviet Union, of course, but it also says something about public discourse. It says something about what people feel is possible and we're a bit bereft, I think.

— **What would you like to see happen, if you had the power? If tomorrow morning we woke up, and Clare's society existed, what would it be like?**

— I want to say two things to that because the kind of transformation I want couldn't be one person - me or anyone else - in power for five years. It would be a society wanting change and working together to bring it about. So much would have to change and we'd have to build it together. So it would be much less unequal, much more participative. I think we've gone mad on consumerism. I don't think it's making people happy. People would start valuing social activities. Of course everyone wants the basics, but after that, we should spend money on people doing things together and being kind to each other and looking after children and old people, and so on. Britain would then have a different role in the world. I think we could be a really constructive player in trying to get a more equally developed, less conflict-ridden world. It would be a safer world and you'd get the levels of international co-operation that are capable of dealing with the crises of climate change and so on. So it would be a happier society. Our country would play a better role and there'd be a better chance for the future of everybody. That's what I want. But no one individual can do that. It has to be a movement of ideas, of people, of hope. I really want electoral reform so that a number of parties would share political power and start to construct it. That's part of it but not the whole of it. We saw the alternative with Obama, you can get the supposedly most powerful role in the world and have very limited power. It's got to be part of something bigger.

— **I wonder if executive power isn't, itself, an essentially masculine idea - the big man at the top who's supposed to fix everything when the truth about power is that it's always diffuse. It's about voluntary engagement and it's about communities wanting to look after themselves and each other.**

— There's something very profound here. The problem with that reality is that people feel powerless and yet the power is in everyone coming together. You need some kind of organisation and the ideas to make people see that they can do it. I think at the moment, all over the world, people feel angry and powerless. They are fed up with what's going on but everyone feels they can't do anything about it. And if you feel you can't do anything, then of course you can't do anything. Governments change but nothing changes very much. Then people just say, 'Politicians are useless.' The danger here is that you end up with some dictator promising to transform everything. That's what history tells us. So it has to be people coming together. Ideas, there have to be ideas in it. And we haven't got that at the moment. It's very odd.

— **Can we talk about you personally, how you would say things that were difficult to hear, but true, and you would become unpopular? There was a time when you were a very unpopular figure because when things aren't working it's not popular to hear they're not working. That's a form of power isn't it, of having the courage to speak up?**

— I did talk about this earlier when you said, 'You're an MP. You have power.' You try to put at the disposal of your constituents the power they've given you in the office. You try to speak the truth, which I think has got power in it, but it's a strange power because you don't always succeed. Yours can be a minority voice. I went to an Al-Jazeera conference the other weekend and people in the Middle East are feeling very depressed. The situation in the region is terrible. I was talking about how - number one - the experts often can't predict what's coming, like all those spies and intelligence agencies didn't know the Soviet Union was going to collapse. They didn't know that the Arab Spring was coming or, more recently, that we were about to have an economic crisis. The Queen asked, when she went to the London School of Economics, 'We've got all these economists, didn't anybody know it was going to happen?' So you can get too clever-dickey about what brings change. Then I was talking about people sneering at us for saying, 'I'm not buying South African oranges.' You know, the beginning of that. I can remember Mrs Thatcher saying in the House of Commons that Nelson Mandela was a terrorist. And then I remember Nelson Mandela coming on a state visit and having the full red carpet treatment at Westminster Hall and Tory MPs rushing over to be in the photo with him. What I was trying to say to people in the Middle East is: if you get too depressed, remember some of these examples where people sneered at you for being on the other side. The Vietnam War is another example but people have to be both right and have the courage to speak up, then they have to organise with others. Individuals cannot do it alone. And that seems to be the bit that isn't working at the moment. At the Middle East conference, it was mostly academics and I was saying that ideas matter but divide and rule is at work, and the region is so weak. I find the treatment of the Palestinians unbearable in its injustice. So I was saying these kinds of things. If you look at examples that have brought about historical change, all the powers that be sneered and didn't participate. Slavery is an example. Everyone says it was William Wilberforce[19] who brought about abolition. But if you look at the history, the Quakers were crucial, both in the US where they helped people escaping from the southern states, and in Britain where they mobilised public opinion. Yes, Wilberforce did his job of putting it in the House of Commons, but the lead for saying, 'This is intolerable,' came from ordinary people coming together and making a stand. So that's my understanding of how history works and I think we've lost that understanding and that's why we're disempowered. Now freedom means: you can go shopping!

— **You have never shied away from saying what needed to be said, even if it might have personal consequences. That's a kind of courage. And there's power in courage. Can you acknowledge that or is it a fantasy that I've inferred and you were just getting on with it?**

— In Britain, in politics, the media are a monstrous burden. *The Sun* went for me and it hurts. You feel surrounded and it affects other people close to you. So I was well aware of those kind of attacks right from the beginning. I was attacked for calling out that minister who was sneeringly talking about equality for women. I said, 'I know you're not allowed to say people are drunk, but I'm sure he's got a problem.' And he denied it and later admitted it.[20] I was attacked for saying early on, 'I think they've got the wrong people for the Birmingham pub bombing.'[21] Yes, I think it's just temperamentally the way I am but it doesn't mean it's not hard. In a sense it's not courage because that's just how I am. If you know what I mean?

— **It would be courage for me because I'm not really like that. I'm Mr Non-Confrontation.**

— But you would find your own way then.

— **Hopefully.**

— There are different ways of doing it. You can do it in your art. I mean you see a lot of radicalism in art and the theatre. I think again it's a bit muddled at the moment, even though there are lots of people trying to say things. I'm not sure what it's amounting to. That's the other thing. We need all the different people with all the different personalities and talents. No one thing is the best. The whole idea of IQ is a distortion. You know, some people have artistic, musical, engineering, mathematical skills. I think your description of me is true. I think in politics often one's strengths and weaknesses are linked. I can't help it, if something is not true, I feel the need to speak out and say it and you get brickbats, but that's my strength. But then the weakness is, I don't know, you don't fit in and slither up the greasy pole all the time. On the other hand, I got to be in the Cabinet. I got to run a wonderful department and influence the international system doing it my way. That's not bad.

— **Maybe that's a really wonderful definition of power - not to do it someone else's way. True power is finding your own way to approach the mission you need to fulfil.**

— It's Shakespeare, isn't it? Hamlet. 'To thine own self be true.' I think there's a thing now, about what makes a human being satisfied. We've only got this time on this earth and I think that 'to thine own self be true' is profoundly important for being comfortable in your own skin. And we should have a society where people can be true to themselves and make a contribution and not have to be fitted into somebody else's straightjacket. But it was a long time ago when Shakespeare wrote that. Those words are spoken by that awful man in Hamlet, the father of the young woman, Ophelia, who Hamlet loves but who dies. It's her father and he's a bit of a creep in the play, but he says those words as advice to his son when he's going to France. And he says various things: 'Neither a lender nor a borrower be. But to thine own self be true.' A long time ago. Do people say that to kids at school anymore? I think they say, 'Jump through these hoops. Jump through hoops! Jump through hoops!'

— **Get your score. Pass your tests.**

— Not, 'What do you really care about? What are you good at? What do you believe? What do you think?' I don't think that's in education anymore. 'Be a clone.'

— **I think that's long gone. It wasn't there when I was at school even.**

— No, but there was more messy space to explore these things in. It's even more driven now. Jump through hoops! Jump through hoops!

— **I'm really struck by Rudolph Steiner[22] and his approach to education. Steiner said, 'Every child is a genius and it's the job of education to find it'. And I thought that was such a beautiful statement. The child is at the centre and everything else is structure and scaffolding.**

— I had a young mother come and live with me for a time. She was stuck for somewhere to live. When you're a bit older, seeing a little child grow, it's miraculous. And we've all done it. But when they learn, roll, crawl, walk, eat. It's just beautiful. Every single human being does that and we are losing that sense of wonder.

— **Can I ask you about the text I sent over? I'm really interested in the militancy of those suffragette women. I think it was Caroline Lucas, on social media, who said something like, 'The danger is that everything about the Women's Movement is being sanitised and turned into 'those nice women who fought for the vote in a socially acceptable way' and we should not take away from the power, the profundity, of their militant action.' Whatever you think of it, they had the courage to get themselves arrested. They were force fed. Mary Jane Clarke died because of force feeding. She was the first woman to die for the vote - this incredible militancy. They were, as I understand it, very careful to avoid harming anybody. They focused on property. I read a piece where Emmeline Pankhurst asked for volunteers to bomb MPs' houses. But the people mustn't be in. They've got to be out. And they must cause damage to the property only to say, 'You're not listening to us, you male MPs.' And they had twelve people volunteer to do it. Now I wouldn't have had the courage, I don't think.**

— Is it courage? I think you're absolutely right that if they march and make their demands and they are completely ignored over and over again, then they've got to think of some more abrasive tactics. But there is a big moral question about those tactics. Breaking the windows of government offices, it seems to me, is a completely reasonable sort of escalation. But setting fire to postboxes, I don't like it because there's some ordinary folk writing a letter to their mum with a five pound note in it (well not five pounds in those days but you know what I mean). If you look at all protest movements, anger does produce people who will go to greater and greater extremes. Do you remember the poll tax? There were demonstrations all over the country including, I remember, Stroud and Gloucester. And then there was a march in Trafalgar Square and it turned very violent. I'm sure some of those who went towards violence would say they are the ones that changed the law. I think that's not true. I think that it was a culmination. In general, there is a place in history for the use of violence to resist oppression. It's recognised in international law as an entitlement. But I think you can only use it if it can work, because violence is always ugly. I admire the suffragettes' courage. But I think it's wrong to think you can bomb people's houses and everyone will be out. The chances that the servants or the children will be there are enormous. Do you remember the Angry Brigade?[23] They were a small group in Britain in the Seventies, I think, and they tried to bomb Robert Carr's house.[24] He was the Home Secretary at the time. I don't think they got very far. Or think of the Baader-Meinhof gang.[25] They killed people. It's morally questionable and it didn't work in those cases because it doesn't enthuse other people. The courage of the suffragettes in going to prison and going on hunger strike and being force fed is incredible. And I think it was very brutal in those days and lots of them had permanent damage. I admire that and feel for them. But I think the use of violent protest always must be very properly morally judged.

— **It's very dangerous isn't it? The territory is extremely dangerous.**

— Because you could end up bombing the MPs' houses and the children were there or the servants. That's not right. In two senses. In pure moral terms and in terms of the popularity of your cause. I think it was the Mayor of Cork who went on hunger strike in the resistance in Ireland or one of those Irish leaders of rebellion. I can't remember exactly what he said, but it's something like, 'They can't take from us our power to suffer and endure.'[26] And there is a power in that, there really is. Because those women being on hunger strike, and what they suffered, I'm sure moved people enormously, more than the broken windows, although one flowed from the other. So in those texts that you've sent me to read, there's the suffragette who went to the meeting of the Liberals and smuggled herself into the box and challenged the whole meeting. I admired that very much. You imagine, thousands of people there and she speaks up and I'm sure it caused some consternation among them because there were people in the Liberal Party who were troubled by the issue. Though they didn't do anything about in the end, Asquith wasn't it? Then there was the call to break windows, and if you're careful about which windows, I wouldn't say it's necessarily bad. I've got doubts about the setting alight of the post because you get some people hurt that are not your enemy. But I don't think that if that was all it was, they would have ever won, like the Angry Brigade and Baader Meinhof, if you like. They used violence and went to prison and fizzled out and got nowhere. The cause was just, there was lots of support, there were different forms of mobilisation. But again, it's like Wilberforce and slavery, there's the myth that Emmeline Pankhurst did it all on her own and her poor followers just marched behind her. You wouldn't have got the transformation that way.

— **There were many male supporters of the movement as well, weren't there?**

— One of the things I absolutely love and I think has not been stressed enough in this year of commemoration is that working-class men also gained the vote for the first time. There had been long campaigns in Britain from the Chartists[27] onward to get the vote. All those young men had gone and risked their lives (or sacrificed their lives) in that awful war and they were not allowed to vote. It was unbearable. They had to give them the vote. And they also gave it to women over thirty; the argument was if you give it to all women, there'd be more women than men voting and that wouldn't do. So the big advance for women included this advance for working-class men. Now, we're not marking that. I think this is a really important aspect because it's an example where a proper, radical move forward for women is not just 'women up, men down', it's something better that includes everybody. So, I'm going around your question of their resort to violence. I admire non-violent resistance. There's this famous quote: '...but the fools, the fools, the fools! - they have left us our Fenian dead, and while Ireland holds these graves, Ireland unfree shall never be at peace.'[28] It's about the capacity to endure and take the violence, the hurt your enemy inflicts on you. You see it in Gandhi and that famous film about the salt marches. It's the pure beating of people who are protesting. We saw it in Martin Luther King and the whole civil rights movement. That was all peaceful and we still can see pictures of people being beaten. Even now when I think of it, it makes me flinch. So there's an enormous power in resisting, maybe going beyond the law but not being violent. Then it's the state that is violent and then people of moral conscience find it unbearable and your cause wins more ground. There are always moral dilemmas in violent resistance. There are people who say, 'Oh, let's have a revolution!' when they want social change. But if you look at the history of revolutions, they only come when societies are in the deepest trouble - the French Revolution, and the Russian Revolution, for example - and it takes a long time for them to make progress. They cause so much violence and brutality. It's not the best way to achieve change. That's going a bit beyond the suffragettes. Was it Emily Davison who went to pull the reigns of the king's horse? As I understand it, she wasn't going to commit suicide, she was going to put a suffragette banner on the horse or something. But clearly there are some people who are so passionate they will go farther than others and some of that is just in the nature of human beings. But if a movement is going to advocate the use of force - well I think it shouldn't plan the use of force except in international situations of resisting pressure, but that's another argument. You can plan to resist by breaking the law and taking the consequences and enduring the suffering. That takes enormous courage, more than breaking something and running away. In fact wasn't that in the texts you sent me? Someone secretly setting light to post boxes and then running away. But then she did declare herself.

— **She was trying to get arrested and the police wouldn't take her in.**

— That's right, so that's an interesting question.

— **Part of the point of breaking the windows or setting fire to the letter boxes was to have broken the law in order then to be sent to prison and then to demand political prisoner status. That way the cause was amplified in the public imagination.**

— Absolutely. And of course we saw exactly the same thing in Northern Ireland. Bobby Sands got elected as an MP while he was on hunger strike.[29] I remember that helped to create the atmospherics producing more determination to get a peace process. But it's an example of enduring suffering rather than attacking someone. And that's Gandhi and Martin Luther King. If you look at the suffragettes from that point of view we might say, 'Bit dodgy on the post boxes but the willingness to break the law and take the consequences and to be seen to suffer for your cause is very powerful and takes enormous courage.' This is true of the suffragettes and

Gandhi movement for the independence of India. There was a small violent movement in India but it wasn't the powerful one, which is also interesting. Obviously the IRA used violence but probably the hunger strikers moved more mountains than bombs. So, you might have assumed that I would just respond well to the idea of 'the more radical the better' but it's more complicated than that. Being willing to break the law when the law is impossibly unfair is a perfectly moral, right thing to do, but you need a lot of people doing it to have an impact. But the use of violence against others is to be ruled out, I think, except in resisting oppression in that kind of conflict situation. Look at the Baader Meinhof gang, I mean, what were they doing it for? The extremeness of violence absolutely destroys any strength in the cause. Yes, working-class men got the vote too and Emeline Pankhurst ended up being a Tory candidate. Remember that? Amazing! And Sylvia ended up being a darling of the emperor of Ethiopia and her son grew up there and became a historian of Ethiopia and is either still alive or just died very recently. You know, she was the lefty one of the daughters.[30]

— **I'd like to pick up on the vote for working-class men. When we first met, you said something that struck me powerfully. It was an aside really. You were talking about capitalism and Britain and what's** happening with employment and you said, 'There is a shortage of really good quality working-class jobs.' And I had never heard 'working class' and 'good quality jobs' put together. I had always heard the idea that the working class was about trying to elevate yourself out of it. I realised, when you talked about good quality working-class work, that you saw a nobility in working and in being a working person. And that it wasn't that you were working class because you couldn't be somewhere else, it was because it was a good place to be. I've heard it expressed many, many years ago, when I was very little probably, but since then, with the rise of Thatcherism and this kind of very aggressive capitalism, it's always been about how everyone wants to be upwardly mobile and wants to be the CEO of something. I wondered if you would talk more about the idea of what the working class means to you?

— Marx's insight was that capitalism was creating this new class of workers in factories that had great potential power. They could organise and that would be an engine of historical change. Of course it was nothing to do with something like the Soviet Union, that hadn't yet become industrialised. He understood that capitalism had crises of boom and bust and that's what he thought would create this revolutionary possibility, but he also understood that capitalism created fantastic technology. It was very creative, but it was unfair in the way things were distributed. So he imagined that this revolution would come when all the good creativity in capitalism would be used for the benefit of everybody. So he wasn't saying 'stop capitalism', he was saying 'manage it in a way that doesn't cause crises and that brings everyone benefits' and of course in those days it was much harsher. Not that Marx is the only insight, but I think it is true that the change to capitalism and the creation of industrialisation made it possible for workers to organise for power, to strike and so on, and that was the great transformative energy in the 20th Century. It culminated in 1945 in a Keynesian-type management of capitalism: less unequal, less crisis-prone, better welfare state, better conditions for working people. It was a more dignified society. But I think we are now past that era because of technology. There are factories in China where, though trade unions are controlled by the state, there have been movements among workers that have led to increases in their wages, which is quite interesting. But in our kind of society that power of organisation among working-class people is very weak now, partly deliberately weakened, but partly because of technological organisation.

So back to the dignity of work. Some of that work in factories might not have had that much dignity but there was some kind of dignity in everyone coming together and demanding fair wages and decent hours. Read the Factory Acts going back a bit further and the Shaftesbury Commission.[31] One thing I remember is about parents staying up all night in order to wake their children to go to the factory at five o'clock in the morning. So it was an enormous struggle to transform that. It didn't just drop out of the sky or out of the goodness of somebody's heart. It was the organisation of working-class people that led to transformation. So that's a big, powerful, incredibly important set of forces that gave to you and I the kind of more comfortable society that we were born into and grew up in and they should all be given respect for what they achieved for themselves and for just a more civilised way of living.

There is dignity in work. I said my grandad was a toolmaker. It is very skilled work. He used to carve out the centre of pennies and put them together and give them to us. Little things like that take a lot of skill. I mean it's not of value, it's just the pure admiration of the skill that fascinates a child. If I take my car to have its MOT, I'll go to a local garage and there are guys who've worked there for years and they know all about cars and I don't know about cars and I respect them and they know that they've got some knowledge that people need. It's not just a job and I think that's how work should be. I remember the workers in the car industry when I was young. They were just standing on the track, doing a repetitive job. That is not satisfying work but the wages were fantastic. That was the first of the working class who had cars and went on holiday to Spain and had mortgages etc but became very militant. Now you've got these beautiful robots doing the work. So there is repetitive work that is not fulfilling but in that case, they got very good wages and had good status in society and an enjoyable job through their organisation. I think a lot of coal miners, although that's a terribly harsh job, had a fantastic sense of solidarity and pride. So obviously nowadays, if we still had deep mines (and coal's bad for the environment anyway) but just for example, probably technology could cut it. But even with that most awful kind of work, the organisation of coal miners and what they built, produced fantastically dignified communities. It's the same with steel workers - this is one of the things that has happened in Wales and the North East and so on that's left people with jobs in bars and shops and Amazon warehouses and a lot of those working-class men have lost their dignity. There is a lot of skill in lots of work, like people who paint houses. Can you paint a house? You've got to know how to clean it off, what kind of paint to use. If you don't know these things, the house will fall apart. I have to find people who can help me do jobs to sort out my house. I had a broken window and I needed someone to fix the window and put some bars on it. I'd ring up people and say, 'Can you do this?' And then one man said, 'Yes, I can do that.' Well, bless him. I need him. He can do something I can't do. And then it's that: the labourer is worthy of his hire. Because he should get a decent wage for doing that. You can't do it. I can't do it. I remember years ago I got in a taxi in Whitehall. I was a young MP and this taxi driver said, 'I suppose you're going to a meeting?' I don't think he knew I was an MP. I said, 'Yes I am.' He said, 'I don't know. Everyone's going to meetings. I don't know who's doing any work anymore. We all used to go to factories and make things and now you're all going to meetings!' And if you take other work, like caring for the frail or elderly, it's very badly paid. It's not respected. It's really important work.

Now people are talking about artificial intelligence and we're running out of work. And yet we've got a growing elderly population and we've got absolutely no way of caring enough for the frail and sick elderly. There's plenty of work there. We could do better with children. What is it? We learn half of what we ever learn before we're five. So we should be pouring love and attention and chances to be creative into all our little ones but nursery workers are paid very little. My father used to say when we went on holiday to Ireland, if someone was working, he would say, 'God bless the work.' You know if someone was fixing up the thatch on a house etc. I think there should be dignity in work. We do have meaning in work. I'm sure you have meaning in your work. I wouldn't want to do nothing and have servants doing everything and you just sit around being rich and lazy.

— **That's why the rich all seem to end up taking lots of drugs and getting divorced.**

— Yes. And we should organise work with its dignity and when there is tedious work to be done, you can organise it in ways that people get respect out of doing it. I think that's one of the things that's gone wrong and that's causing so much disgruntlement. Even in the tough work of the North East and Wales and so on, there was some dignity in organisation and the pay and the pension and now that's all gone - no dignity, not much pay and no pension.

— **Power doesn't always have to be aggressing, pushing yourself forward, the archetypal male paradigm of power as oppression and domination,**

and trampling on people to get to the top.

— Which also traps a lot of men who just don't like that way of behaving. Then they're told, 'You're not a proper man then, because you're not like that.' Whereas it would be more helpful to say, 'I'll come and see if you're a good leader if I find a happy, inclusive, highly effective organisation.' That's real leadership and I believe it goes together, that if you include people and they can make a contribution, you can make a more creative, more productive organisation. It's not like, be kind and it's less efficient, be nasty and it's more efficient. I don't believe that's true.

This current model of leadership in business with lots of financial incentives is producing leadership that maximises short-term shareholder value, rather than investing in research and development and so on. It's one of the things that's going wrong with capitalism, creating 'shareholder value', giving money back to shareholders, but not creating anything new. There's now serious commentary about this from people who look at business efficiency. Shareholder value may go up but is that really measuring value for the society and indeed for the company. If you don't do any research and development and don't invest in creating anything new, in the end the thing will shut down. Look at some of the companies we've seen just go to the wall. Was it

Eastman or Kodak? You know with the changes in technology, big old companies just fold. Now if they'd been closer to what was happening, they would have diversified and taken in the new technologies etc. This emphasis on maximising shortterm shareholder value is making capitalism uncreative. Productivity is low. It's a phenomenon across the economy. Increased productivity means a more productive economy and people are perplexed about why productivity is dropping. I think it's linked to this emphasis on shareholder value - just pump up shortterm shareholder value, get rid of people and then you're not replenishing anything. You can go to the wall. The big new companies like Google, Amazon, Apple etc are the biggest companies in the world, but that's a bit odd. Yes, Apple products are good but it's not the only thing we need. These companies are awash with capital that they can't invest. Of course they have clever people who put it all together, but they are really successful because of a breakthrough in computer technology which came out of American Defence R&D.

— **You really couldn't make it up, could you?**

— No, it's fantastic.

— **Can I ask you one more question which is very personal but see what you think. I was looking on your website and I was looking at the photographs** of when you retired from being the MP for Birmingham Ladywood. When I looked at all the pictures, there were two things that struck me. Everyone was there - tiny kids and very old people and imams and bishops and they all loved you. You could see that everyone just loved you. Of course you left the Labour Party and these people just carried on voting for you because they wanted you, and that strikes me as incredible personal power. You also said that one of the things you were proudest of was your constituency work and you felt that nowadays MPs didn't take it seriously enough or didn't acknowledge the value of it enough. I felt that was somehow connected up with this incredible power of truthfulness and integrity and being real and people knowing you were real. I think the question is: isn't that the ultimate power because they just loved you? Except for the Tory voters obviously. They didn't love you.

— Well some Tories come up to me and say, 'I would never vote for you but..!' I think that's connected to my point about how you can't be altruistic in order to be loved and respected because then it's not altruism. Isn't there a saying that virtue is its own reward? I mean, you get all the knocks and bashes but people are very fair and I think there is some reward in a human life beyond the material. Respect and affection from other people is, in a way, the deepest reward. Obviously in our personal relationships we have love and we fall out of love or whatever and we need to be loved in our family etc. But there's a broader thing in your work and in society, and if you get that affection and respect it's deeply, deeply, deeply rewarding.

People are so fair, even when you can't win everything for them, if they know you tried. I really enjoyed my constituency. It was hard work but all that human life is there and you get to know everybody and understand what's going on for them. I used to ask asylum seekers how much they paid to get here, so I have a real understanding of the criminal people-smugglers that are part of the system that needs fixing. I enjoyed all of that work. But sometimes now, when I'm driving through the constituency, I think, 'Oh I'd be going to the advice bureau now,' and there's a little bit of relief that I don't have to still keep doing it. And the other thing that happened is they brought in big allowances so MPs could have an office in the constituency. Then they have staff who see most of the people and I think this is a mistake because we should have Citizens' Advice Bureaux that are funded and law centres. The MP's office shouldn't become an alternative place to take your problems. There should be other systems and then going to the MP should be more personal, so the MP does the service, but also learns.

— **I was going to say, surely MPs need to see their constituents otherwise they don't really know what's going on with people. Otherwise what are they representing? Just an idea that's getting more and more out of date as they don't interact with people.**

— And they come from a narrower section of society in all parties. It goes some way to explaining Brexit and Trump. Politics isn't picking up all this anger and resentment which then expresses itself in these rather dramatic decisions. It's a kind of protest. Politics should be listening to people from those communities who are voicing their anger. Politics is failing, so you get some other force coming into play. I do think that if we don't do better there is a real danger that things will become more populist, more fascistic, there'll be more conflict. There's a danger we're going that way. People say, 'Are we in the Thirties?' I wonder, 'Are we in the Twenties?' Are we just having fun and drinking too much and having drugs and buying too much and being obsessed with sex and sexual relationships while everything goes to hell. And the dictators come later. History never quite repeats itself, but I think you can learn by reflecting on it and I don't think we're learning very much at the moment. You see the anger and people are totally perplexed by it. However your point was, it is a reflection of power that you can do things that make people love you. That's an unusual way of looking at power and you can't make people love you. You can do things where people give you love and respect and that's very satisfying.

— **That's also very different as an idea. I was struck so powerfully by it from all the pictures of your leaving party. It was extraordinary, I thought.**

— Of course, the ones who come to the party are the ones who like you.

ANNIE KENNEY

Ann 'Annie' Kenney (13 September 1879 - 9 July 1953) was an English working-class suffragette who became a leading figure in the Women's Social and Political Union. During a Liberal rally at the Free Trade Hall, Manchester, in October 1905, Kenney and Christabel Pankhurst interrupted a political meeting attended by Winston Churchill and Sir Edward Grey to shout: 'Will the Liberal government give votes to women?'

After unfurling a banner declaring 'Votes for Women' and shouting, they were thrown out of the meeting and arrested for causing an obstruction; Pankhurst was taken into custody for a technical assault on a police officer after she spat at him to provoke an arrest. Kenney was imprisoned for three days for her part in the protest. The incident is credited with inaugurating a new phase in the struggle for women's suffrage in the UK with the adoption of militant tactics.

Emmeline Pankhurst wrote in her autobiography that 'this was the beginning of a campaign the like of which was never known in England, or for that matter in any other country ... we interrupted a great many meetings ... and we were violently thrown out and insulted. Often we were painfully bruised and hurt'. Kenney and Minnie Baldock formed the first London branch of the WSPU in Canning Town in 1906, holding meetings at Canning Town

Public Hall. In June that year Kenney, Adelaide Knight, and Mrs Sparborough were arrested when they tried to obtain an audience with H. H. Asquith, then Chancellor of the Exchequer. Offered the choice of six weeks in prison or giving up campaigning for one year, Kenney chose prison, as did the others.

TRANSCRIPT

Annie Kenney speaking at a meeting of the Women's Social and Political Union at the Albert Hall, London, 19 March 1908.

Mrs Pankhurst, women of Great Britain, who are here to demand the just liberties of a nation, and who have a great consciousness of right at heart, I want to thank you on behalf of Mrs Pankhurst and of those women who have been away, for your grand support, and for your true loyalty to this Union while we women were in prison. You do not know, you cannot understand what it means to we women workers and organisers of this Union, how full our hearts feel of joy, full of hope, full of confidence, and our souls full of inspiration, to see you support our great Women's Movement. I cannot help but feel glad to be once again in the Albert Hall. Almost two years ago when the Liberals of the country had decided to hold the meeting of the century in the Royal Albert Hall, we women of Manchester agreed with Mrs Pankhurst that one of we women ought to come to London, get tickets if humanly possible, come to the meeting, and see if Women's Franchise was included in the great reform. I was the one who was sent to be the delegate from the Manchester branch. We were very fortunate - we always are - we got 4 tickets; two for Mr John Burns' private Box - unknown to Mr Burns [laughter], and two for the orchestra. It was decided that one of the London women and I should occupy the box. The night came for the meeting, so I sent a letter to the leading Liberal man, saying that I was inside the Hall, that I hoped that Women's Suffrage would be treated in the manner that it well deserved and would be included in the great Liberal programme. I also said that, if it was not included in the programme, I should feel bound to get up and make a protest against its exclusion. We women were like the Barons in the Saga of King John, we had sworn that the women of this country should have their political liberty, and that we as women would declare war against any government that was run on unconstitutional lines. We have done it. Now, you all know that women's suffrage was not included in the programme. So, when I saw the speakers were getting to the end of their speeches I got up in the box, when they were telling of the great reforms that the Liberals were going to do, and I said to them, 'Are you going to give women the Vote?' The whole hall seemed to rise and much to the dismay of Mr John Burns and his friends I pulled out my banner from under my cloak and hung it over the box. I shall never forget the scene. There seemed to be thousands of people against me, but I didn't mind, because I knew that we had done the right thing, and I knew that our action that night was like summer rain on a drooping flower, it would give new life, new spirit to the women's movement in London, and is not this meeting one of the many proofs that we women were right? One cannot help but wonder all about the old reformers who have gone by, and I often wonder what they must have felt about their reforms, what they must have felt about their movements, and knowing that every reform that strove for liberty, that worked against oppression and slavery, that worked for the up-lifting of the human race, was won more through pressure than from a sense of justice - was won at a price of human sacrifice and human life. Think how the men won their first Franchise Reform; think how the Merchants Shipping Bill was won to save thousands of honest seamen from death; think how the first Factory Acts were won, to protect the lives of our little children against the greed of employers, and save their little bodies from this cruel machine; think of all the strife and loss of life before the government of that day would recognise the need of combination between the workers to protect their interests. The strife of those days won for us the liberties we now enjoy, the strife of today will win liberty and freedom for the generations that are to come. I do not think when the battle is won we shall ever have cause to regret all the uphill work that had to be done, but we shall rather think of what we should have missed had we got our Vote without a great struggle for it. We should not have had, we should not have known our dear leader Mrs Pankhurst, we should not have known our champion, Miss Christabel Pankhurst, we should not have had our treasure of treasurers, Mrs Pethick Lawrence and I should have been far poorer without them. They would not have had you good women, there would not have been the grand fellowship existing between the women of every class, of every creed, as there is today. To the Liberal Party is the loss, to the women of our land will come the gain. Let us just look at the conditions the people of our land are living under today. Just think, and then be satisfied with life as it is if you can! Your prisons are full, your workhouses are overcrowded, your lunatic asylums are overcrowded, you have over thirteen million starving women, men and children, you have your thousands of underpaid, sweated women workers, and we want to consider what all this means to we women! Have you ever been in our British Institutions? Have you been in your workhouses and seen your old women packed together, just at the time of life when they should be made bright and comfortable for their old age, to give those tired hands and weary hearts a chance of rest? Have you ever been in our maternity wards? And seen our young girl mothers? Have you ever been in our imbecile wards, and seen the children that are borne of women, some of the children that are borne in sin? It would be wrong if the women were satisfied; it would be wrong if we women did not burn with righteous indignation. Where is our religion, where is our

Christianity, if we are prepared to stand by without lifting our hands to help? Let us look at the condition of our prisons...

SPECIAL BRANCH REPORT

On Annie Kenney's speech at a suffragette meeting, Essex Hall, The Strand, London, 31 January 1913.

Miss A. Kenney opened her speech by referring to the Labour Conference, and made an attack on the Labour Party. Continuing she said, 'They have not promised any more than what Mr. Balfour promised in 1907. We demand that the Labour Party shall vote against the Government, not on the Franchise Bill alone, but on every question that comes up in the House of Commons, until they have voted them out of Office. This is our campaign:- We have got to turn the Government out. At every street corner and place where we have public meetings we must instil into the minds of the public that unless the Government gives way, and brings in a Bill to enfranchise women, we must make everyone talk of turning the Government out. We have got to have it ringing in the minds of everyone in the country - Turn the Government out! Turn the Government out!

'What have we to do? We have got to fight on. I should like to see a sandwich board going all over London, and on the top marked, 'Wanted! Some good window smashers'. That is what we want. You know that every woman ought never to go out without a hammer in her pocket, and never to go out, at least without touching one pillar box. You, who cannot break windows, for goodness sake get on with something else. Everyone can do a pillar box, for you must remember that that is the one thing that touches the pockets of the people. How do they know their letters are going to be destroyed? They don't know when their pillar box is going to be attacked, therefore, it is the duty of every suffragist and suffragette to go on attacking every pillar box throughout the country, and breaking every window they can without being caught. What we have to do is, we have not to say, 'Oh, only 50 arrests!' But, 'Thank goodness only 50 of them caught! And here we are thousands of us.'

'Don't let us be too keen on getting arrested, but get off if we can, and do some more damage. It is no good women thinking of other people doing it. It is your duty, every woman in this audience not only to sympathise with militancy, it is your duty to create such a situation, that unless you all take your part in creating that situation, that situation will not be created. […]

'Women of our union, let us make London absolutely unbearable for the average citizen, until the average citizen along with the shopkeepers will go on a deputation and fill Charing Cross to Palace Yard with people, to tell the Government that women shall have the vote at once.

'We can easily do it. Come out in numbers! So when you go home to-night think of what scheme you can do, and go and do it; lose no time, but get on with your business. It will have more effect on the men in the street than any public meeting you can hold. We have got to hold meetings, but the only thing you have got to be is militant! Militant! And more militant!!!'

PLEASANCE PENDRED

Pleasance Pendred was an active member of the Women's Social and Political Union (WSPU). She was arrested on 28 January 1913 for smashing the windows of an antique shop at 167 Victoria Street in Westminster. She was sentenced to four months' imprisonment and hard labour. In prison, she went on hunger strike for at least two months. She was force-fed and became ill as a consequence.

She received a hunger strike medal from the WSPU acknowledging her bravery and commitment to the cause of Votes for Women.

Pendred had been a teacher at a London school for more than 25 years, resigning shortly before her window smashing. Little else was known about her until the recent discovery that Pleasance Pendred was most likely an alias and her real name was probably Kate Pleasance Jackson.

Kate adopted her alias consistently throughout her militant activism as a suffragette. Her cover name was also adopted by suffragette newspapers and the character witnesses at her trial, including the principal of her old school and the local Reverend F.M. Green. The engraving on her hunger strike medal is also dedicated to Pleasance Pendred.

After her release from prison in 1913, she continued to speak at her local WSPU branch. She is last recorded as a speaker for the North Islington (formerly Hornsey) WSPU branch meeting in August 1913.

In later life, she moved to Sussex and died in Lewes in 1948.

WHY WOMEN TEACHERS BREAK WINDOWS

A defence by Pleasance Pendred, member of the Women's Social and Political Union. (Pamphlet first published c.1912 by the Woman's Press.)

Gentlemen, I want you to see that I am not the kind of woman to break civil laws without a strong conscientious motive. You will, therefore, pardon my telling you that I have led a blameless life. For more than 25 years I have been class mistress in one of the large London schools. In January last, when I sent in my resignation, I received proof of the deepest appreciation from my colleagues, superiors, and employers. It is with the greatest repugnance that I realise that no constitutional method will bring Woman Suffrage. We women believe that the vote, used as we women mean to use it, will be a mighty aid in preventing moral evils.

I think that any of you would look forward with dread to forcible feeding as carried on, not in our hospitals, but in our prisons. Well, I declare to you that the idea of lifting my hand in cool determination to destroy was a more dreadful idea than that of forcible feeding. You little know how we women have to screw up and screw up our courage to acting point.

The Principle of the Thing

Mrs. Pankhurst is not responsible for my deed. While I love and honour her as a woman, she might have talked for an eternity and not have moved me to militancy. It is the truths she tells; truths that I have proved in my own life; such things as child outrage. We hear of Homes filled with outraged children only, and that these Homes are insufficient.

The Society for the Prevention of Cruelty to Children state that 807 children treated immorally passed through their hands last year - that is more than two per day. Last February, a schoolmaster, whom I have known, was found guilty of indecently assaulting eleven of his schoolchildren, most of them under seven years of age. He assaulted these children not once, but for a period of six months.

He was given eighteen months in the second division. The very next month, a suffragist, for breaking glass valued at 3s, was given two months in the third division, with hard labour.

Apologies to Criminals

The judge, in giving sentence to the schoolmaster, said he had considered the schoolmaster's status and social position, and apologised that he could not give him less. Will the gentlemen on the bench today consider my social status - the same, mind you - as the schoolmaster's? Will they give me as little as they can? Will they apologise that they gave me as much?

Can you wonder that we women hold the gentlemen on the Bench in a great and wholesome contempt; for they give malicious sentences, either to grovel to the powers that be, or to pander to wrong public opinion? You may break our bodies, but you can never break this determined spirit to win liberty and justice. I know that I have an overflowing abundance of strength from on High to help me through all that may come. I should like to add that the officials at the police station were very kind to me.

CONSTANCE LYTTON

Lady Constance Georgina Bulwer-Lytton (12 January 1869 - 2 May 1923), usually known as Constance Lytton, was an influential British suffragette activist, writer, speaker and campaigner for prison reform, votes for women, and birth control. She sometimes used the name Jane Warton.

Although born and raised in the privileged ruling class of British society, Lytton rejected this background to join the Women's Social and Political Union (WSPU), the most militant group of suffragette activists campaigning for votes for women.

She was subsequently imprisoned four times, including once in Walton gaol in Liverpool under the nom de guerre of Jane Warton, where she was force-fed while on hunger strike. She chose the alias and disguise of Jane Warton, an 'ugly London seamstress', to avoid receiving special treatment and privileges because of her family connections: she was the daughter of a viceroy and the sister of a member of the House of Lords. She wrote pamphlets on women's rights, articles in The Times newspaper, and a book on her experiences, *Prisons and Prisoners*, which was published in 1914.

While imprisoned in Holloway during March 1909, Lytton used a piece of broken enamel from a hairpin to carve the letter 'V' into the flesh of her breast, placed exactly over the heart. 'V' for Votes for Women.

Lytton remained unmarried because her mother refused her permission to marry a man from a 'lower social order', while she refused to contemplate marrying anyone else.

Her heart attack, stroke, and early death at the age of 54 have been attributed in part to the trauma of her hunger strike and force-feeding by the prison authorities.

LETTER

Lady Constance Lytton to the Rt. Hon. Reginald McKenna, The Home Office, 8 December 1911.

In a petition which I was recently allowed to send you from Holloway Prison, I called your attention to a matter of injustice connected with the sentences passed on suffrage prisoners at Bow Street Police Court on 24 November. As I have received no acknowledgment of this communication I conclude that, because of my premature release from prison, the petition was not shown to you. The particular point on which I wish to appeal to you is this. In the case of Mrs Leigh, the wife of a working man, every one of her previous convictions was quoted against her, the most was made of her past record, Mr. Muskelt for the prosecution commenting on her case in terms of sweeping condemnation, and she was sentenced to two months imprisonment without the option of a fine. In my case, my previous offences where skimmed over, one conviction was omitted altogether from mention, and I was given a sentence of 14 days with the option of a fine. I know Mrs. Leigh personally. I have the very greatest admiration for her heroic altruism and for the fortitude with which she has endured great and prolonged suffering on behalf of others. The motives of her law-breaking are identical with my own. She has served our militant movement for a longer period than I have, consequently the number of convictions is greater in her case than mine, but there is no act which one has committed on behalf of the women's cause that I have not also committed. On the occasion of our recent charges (November 24th), my actions were more violent than hers and I was responsible for wilful damage to property of which she was innocent. It has unfortunately been characteristic of the treatment of Suffrage prisoners that, both in Police Courts and Prisons, those of us who have influential friends have been treated with comparative leniency, whereas working-class women and women who can count on no supporters in political circles have had the harshest treatment. I am willing to believe that you, sir, are not personally responsible for the recent instances of partiality under your jurisdiction. But these essentially undemocratic specialisations inevitably reflect discredit on the Government of which you are a member, and unless you take steps to counteract them, your consent must be assumed. I appeal to you, in no controversial or carping spirit, but as one Liberal to another, to remedy the injustice of this particular case by reducing the term of Mrs. Leigh's sentence. I should be grateful if you would quickly let me have an answer by Monday. Unless you have any objection, I propose to make public this letter on your reply.

I am, sir,

Yours faithfully,

Constance Lytton.

EMILY DAVISON

Emily Wilding Davison (11 October 1872 - 8 June 1913) was a suffragette who fought ferociously for votes for women in Britain in the early 20th Century.

A member of the Women's Social and Political Union and a militant fighter for her cause, she was arrested on ten occasions, went on hunger strike seven times and was force-fed on 49 occasions.

She died after being hit by King George V's horse, Anmer, at the 1913 Derby when she walked onto the track during the race. Some people believed she was trying to pin a badge about women's rights onto the horse but failed.

Davison grew up in a middle-class family and studied at Royal Holloway College, London, and St Hugh's College, Oxford before taking jobs as a teacher and governess. She joined the WSPU in November 1906 and became an officer of the organisation and a chief steward during marches. She soon became known in the organisation for her daring militant action; her tactics included breaking windows, throwing stones, setting fire to postboxes and, on three occasions, hiding overnight in the Palace of Westminster - including the night of the 1911 census. Her funeral on 14 June 1913 was organised by the WSPU. A procession of 5,000 suffragettes and their supporters accompanied her coffin and 50,000 people lined the route through London;

her coffin was then taken by train to the family plot in Morpeth, Northumberland.

Davison was a staunch feminist and passionate Christian, and considered that socialism was a moral and political force for good.

INCENDIARISM

Emily Davison, handwritten manuscript, 1911. ([?] in the text indicates a word is uncertain or illegible.)

A great protest was made on 21 November 1911 by the WSPU against Mr Asquith's announced intention to bring in a Manhood Suffrage Bill in 1912, and his further expression of opinion that Woman Suffrage could be added as an amendment to that bill if the House so wished, but refusing to put it into the Bill himself, as part of the government measure. This was unpardonable, it was the last straw. The women held a demonstration in Parliament Square which developed into a wholesale smashing of the windows in Whitehall, the Strand, some West End establishments and two newspaper offices. As a result, arrests were made, and had to be taken at Bow Street day by day for three weeks. Sixteen of the cases were put to the Session, as the damage done was over £5's worth. Amongst the others were Lady Constance Lytton and Mary Leigh. The Former, who had done well over £5's worth, was only charged with doing it to the value of £3.17s.5d. and was treated most indulgently in the court by Muskelt and given a fortnight's imprisonment. Mary Leigh also had done nothing but defaced a [?] was [next line illegible]... system of as one of the most troublesome of the [?] and given two months. This made my blood boil. The injustice and snobbery was so great. However I thought that something would be done to avenge it. Nothing was done, and I resolved to take it upon myself to make a protest. This couldn't be done at once, as I was engaged in secretarial work. But soon I resolved to stake all. On 1 December 1911, I gave notice to leave and began laying my plans. I resolved that this time damage should be done that could not be repaired. The next step to window breaking was incendiarism. On 8 December, when I was free, at lunch time I walked down the Strand to Fleet Street. When I arrived at the Fleet Street post office which faces Fetter Lane, I calmly stopped at the big open-mouthed receptacle for London letters, I took out of my pocket a packet of the same size as an ordinary letter. It was of grease-proof paper tied with cotton. Inside was some linen well soaked in kerosene. One corner of the paper was torn so as to let out the kerosene rag ready. To this I calmly applied a match which I had struck on a box of matches, and held it for a second. A small boy was passing by and stopped short on seeing what I was doing. I let the packet, now well alight, go down the receptacle, and threw the matches afterwards. I then quietly walked on down Fleet Street and turned into the first Lyons I came to to get lunch. My heart was beating rapidly, as I felt the boy might have given [?] of me, and also I did not know what would happen. After I had sat there a short time (about 10 to 15 minutes), I heard a long shrill whistle. This was followed by others, and still others. They were not cab whistles, they were too agitated for that, they were clearly police whistles. About ten or so of these sounded, and I thought to myself that my object was accomplished and the letters now well alight. When I had finished lunch I went down Fleet Street... into Fetter Lane. There I at once saw an oily [?] constable being spoken to by a plainclothes man. The thought at once flashed into my mind that the latter was instructing the former to keep his eye on the pillar box nearby. I turned down Fetter Lane towards Fleet Street where I saw facing me the post office. I saw the telegraph boys looking at the very aperture down which I had thrown my packet and matches after. I rejoiced greatly, as taken into consideration with the other two [?], I observed that I had succeeded.

The next day I scanned the papers to see if there was any sign of the authorities looking for the perpetrator of the deed. That day I occupied myself with finding out the various penalties to which I was liable. I found that setting fire to buildings was an offence which rendered the person liable to heavy imprisonment up to penal servitude. But setting fire to post offices or pillar boxes or attempting to do so, meant a penalty not exceeding one year.

On the Sunday I occupied myself with putting my house in order, and with writing two print letters to the Press informing them that I had done the deed, that I expected the authorities were looking for the offender, and that I meant to give myself on Monday at 10.30am, by walking up to the constable nearest to the Fleet Street post office and giving myself up to him. These letters I posted in a pillar box near St. Paul's, and then went in to service there. The service was curiously impressive, it was a Sunday in Advent and all was very solemn, and the sermon was to the fact that a glorious morning awaited the people of God.

On Monday I set out ready. I walked to Fleet Street. When I got near the post office I saw numbers of men, evidently pressmen, about. I walked up to City 183 [the police constable's badge number] and said to him, 'Constable, I set fire to this post office at 1.15pm last Friday, and am ready to surrender myself. He said to me, 'I know of nothing - I cannot arrest you.' Then, 'I should not think of giving you such an advertisement for your cause. You are qualifying for Colney Hatch [a psychiatric hospital].'

Seeing I could do nothing with him, I walked into the Post Office, and asked for the Manager. They took me into the Lady Superintendent. She denied all knowledge of any such deed, and asked for my name and address, which I promptly refused her. Seeing that public authorities did not mean to prosecute, I walked away. Later on I phoned up the Press and explained what had happened.

The thought now in my mind was that I must carry out the protest so strongly that it could not be ignored. I laid my plans accordingly. On Monday night I did not go back to my rooms, but on Tuesday night I did. There waiting for me was a detective whom I at once detected. He was standing near my house and when I appeared he walked along parallel to me, stopped and saw me go [?] in, and was there when I emerged a few minutes later. Now I thought of doing my protest on Wednesday night. Accordingly on leaving the place where I spent the day, I spent time dodging and... to make sure that I was not followed and then went off to some friends. I found that Wednesday night would not be a good time for my deed, and so resolved to do it on Thursday.

On Thursday morning I took a train to London. I got out in the city and walked Citywards, buying a box of matches as [?] I had six packets in my pockets. I meant to do as many pillar boxes which were easier to do undiscovered as were necessary, and then to go... a Post Office in some very public place to be careful all fell out as I had arranged.

My first good chance occurred in Leadenhall Street. Halfway down it, going towards Aldgate, there is on the right hand side a large pillar box, on the pavement. This was an excellent chance as the mouth was round out of sight. I coolly took out a packet, lit it, held it a moment. and put it into the

London [?] mouth. I noted that [?] pillar box would not be cleared for half an hour. Very much pleased I walked [here a large ink stain obscures the rest of sentence].

Then came into the Aldgate District and walked about there some time but decided to do nothing as the people were all of the poorer class. I... at last to the Mansion House. In the wall of what I think is Poultney, facing the Mansion House and... Webb is a pillar box let into the wall. I took out a packet, lit it alight. It flared up most splendidly, so that a man coming towards me saw it. He stopped and [?] most amazed, I feared might give me away to a police officer standing near by... I also thought that probably he would be busy and not anxious to waste his time going to charge me and having to spend perhaps several days at police courts. My surmise proved to be right. I walked quietly up Cheapside. I saw a Putney bus on the other side, crossed over, got into it and went west. I went inside and for some time did not feel comfortable as the bus moved slowly. But when I got to Holborn I climbed up on top and began to enjoy myself.

It was a lovely day. I got down at Hyde Park Corner and then walked to Harrods, and near there I entered a post office, and phoned up the London News office as usual. They answered. I told them I was the suffragette who sent letters to them on Monday. They were at once interested. I told them that I had made up my mind not to be done, that I had that morning fired two pillar boxes in the City... [stain makes writing illegible]... that I next intend to do a Post Office... [ink stain] asked them which they thought would be best to do it... [stain] G.P.O. or Parliament Street [?]. They very agitatedly said they could not possibly give advice. Feeling amused and seeing the truth of this, for they would otherwise have been accessories to my act, I answered, 'Of course not I ought to have thought of that! Well! I shall do my deed to be caught at one or the other between one and two o'clock,' then rang off.

I then went and had a good lunch at Slater's [?] near Knightsbridge and dawdled the time between twelve and one o'clock. At one o'clock I sallied forth. It was a glorious day and I walked to Hyde Park Corner. I looked at the clock. Time seemed to be going on, so I took a bus to Trafalgar Square. There I got down and took another bus down Whitehall. My reason for doing this was that if I walked down I might be spotted by detectives who would probably be on the lookout for me and who might prevent me doing anything at all. As I had said to the Press, I wished to be caught 'in the act'. My bus stopped at Bridge Street. I got down. As I turned into Parliament Street, [?] I first came across Superintendent Wells, who looked at me curiously. I then came right facing

Inspector Powell and Constable 185 City, both in private clothes. They looked at me, but I was glad they were coming towards me, as they could not turn too ostentatiously. I however went on past them up to the Post Office. I stood there, and quickly took out of my pocket one of my kerosene packets, struck a match and lit it deliberately and put it in. That did not burn well, and I was not yet arrested, so I took out another and even more ostentatiously set it alight and tried to put it into the letter box. By this time Powell had seen what I was up to. He reached forward, literally grabbed the thing out of my hand, blew it out, seized me violently and said, 'I knew you would do this, Miss Davison.' Constable 185 City seized me on the other side and they rushed me into Cannon Row Police Station. As we went I called out, 'I am arrested, friends.' They hastily led me along into Scotland Yard into Powell's own room, others following. There they took down particulars of me, and I told them that I had done two in the City first that morning. Looking uneasy, they asked me where. I said I would willingly describe the position of the two, and did so. They then went off to ask what the Post Office authorities wanted done, and I had a long chat with Powell, during which we discussed old events. After about half an hour I was taken over to Cannon Row where several inspectors crowded around me who remembered me. One of them said, 'We have been quite expecting to see you in the House of Commons again.' I replied: 'Yes, I know you have,' having often 'detected the detectives' watching me.' Another asserted that they had heard that I was married and 'had given it all up'. Presently they read a charge to me of putting matches and lighted matter into a pillar box in Parliament Street, and then took me off in a taxi cab with Mrs. Parson the Matron, Inspector Powell and a Post Office official. Arrived at Bow Street, I was taken into the Matron's room and found a strange one there. She was proved to be the sister of the one I knew. My case came on about four o'clock or so, before [the Bow Street magistrate] Sir Albert de Rutzen. I had heard it was Mr. Mershame [?] and was surprised when I saw the other. Powell read out the charges against me. When Sir Albert heard [?] them he said: 'Do you think the woman is in her right mind?' Powell replied, 'I believe so; she has been convicted many previous times.' He also said he might have [?] charges to bring up against me. Sir Albert then remanded me for a week to be kept 'under observation'. I was then taken back to the Matron's room, and by this time the gaoler had promised... through to my friends. In an incredibly short time two arrived whose numbers I had given, very dear old friends in the cause, and with them a young fellow, also devoted to the cause. They got tea in to me. I told one to get some luggage I had left ready, and to send it up to Holloway that night. Presently it was time to go in old Black Maria. I begged to be put near the door, and was [ink stain]. I drove out of the yard, my three friends cheered me, and I waved my handkerchief.

The odd incident of the old drive north was that the constable in the van turned out to be the very one with whom I had driven just a year ago to Holloway in Election time. We went [?] again [?] first to Pentonville to let a wretched-looking boy out, and I and another woman only were left. I asked her what she was in for [?]. She told me. It was the usual charge 'soliciting', and she declared to me she had not been doing it. She looked a refined girl and spoke [?] with an educated voice. I said that I know that many of these cases were 'engineered' by the police to get a conviction.

When we arrived at Holloway I [?] first got out and was taken into the reception ward, but they did not seem to know what to do with me. As I was waiting in the courtyard, my constable and I had a further chat. He said to me, 'You have only to breathe the word 'suffragette' here for them to be terrified out of their wits.' I laughed and replied that we had won this respect by sheer fighting and he replied that he knew. By that time they had made up their mind and took me off to the Remand/Hospital wing. Before I was put in my cell the Matron came to see me. We had a long chat about Strangeways (from which she has been [ink stain] to Holloway), and then she put me into a cell.

This cell was large and airy (as the Matron carefully pointed out to me). It has a very fairly decent bed in [ink stain] it and decent washstand. It was next door but one to the one in which Mrs. Pankhurst had been in October-December, 1908. During my week there, I had a very good time. I had hot water brought me in a basin in the morning, quite decent food, including fish and a pudding at midday. Besides this I went to chapel service with the other suffragettes. I had long chats with Mary Leigh. I also, to my joy, had a suffragette next door to me, who was a splendid companion. I was able to write three letters a day, and after a day or two got plenty of papers, and visits. In short I had the treatment which we all ought to have as political prisoners. I pointed this out to a visiting magistrate, who came in to see us at exercise on the Tuesday.

My next-door neighbour went out Monday, and like a regular comrade, went and looked after my... A newly formed society - The Men's Society For Women's Rights - on hearing that even a breath of suspicion had been raised against my sanity, determined to stand by me through thick and thin. Curiously, [?] a brother of mine, to whom I had written, came to see me and tell me that he would get his own solicitor to defend me. I was pleased and surprised.

At last 21 December arrived. It was a freezing wet day. I hauled my baggage along and got in a growler [cab] with two wardresses. We drove to Bow Street. We arrived punctually at ten o'clock. I passed into the Matron's room. It was my old friend this time, who gave me a hearty welcome. Presently my good prison-comrade arrived to take charge of me, with some violets and white heather, and all kinds of nice things. Then my counsel and solicitor came in. We had a little consultation. I explained to them what I wanted done. My counsel, who was a firm suffragist, understood at once. I knew he understood, for he confessed to me that he was always terribly worried on such occasions. For as a lawyer he wanted to get his client off, as a suffragist he did not want to minimize the offence. Others arrived of my good friends, and soon after noon we went into court. I looked round to see the Court well filled with suffragist friends. I saw a poor woman whom I did not know nod to me and say, 'Cheer up.' I made signs to her that I was all right and smiled at my comrades.

The case proceeded. No... was made of my sanity. (I learned later that my counsel saw the letter which Sir Albert de Rutzen had received from the prison doctor to the effect that I was perfectly all right.) Powell gave his evidence and read my statements. My counsel put several very clear questions to him which brought out the fact that Powell had not been very accurate in his statements. For he declared that I was hiding from the public what I was doing, whereas my counsel obliged [him] to practically confess that I was not hiding it. PC 185 was also called, and the postman who sorted the Fleet Street bag on 8 December, who produced two packets found in the bag. The postman at Parliament Street was also called, and he testified to finding nothing in the bag, and gave evidence when he cleared the box. Then I was asked if I wished to say anything. I said I would like to make a statement and Sir Albert de Rutzen, after warning me that it would be used against me, told me to proceed. I began, but found I had to go very slowly, as the prosecutor was taking it down, and could only write longhand. He probably thought that would put me out, but it did not. Very slowly, loudly and clearly I said the following [written separately in a more formal style]:

Gentlemen of the jury, I stand here for justice, although I feel that it is impossible to expect perfect justice in a court where every single official person from the judge to the public is composed of men only. Nevertheless I consider that I have a better chance of justice here where I am tried before 'twelve good men and true' than in the courts where I have been lately tried where the prisoner could neither hear nor be heard, and where he was tried by a judge who was not in the most complete possession of his faculties. I mean no disrespect to English police courts but it seems to me that just as the country insists upon being served by men who are in their prime in the army and navy, so too it should be served by men in their prime in the administration of justice. You have already heard the reasons why I felt bound to adopt this strong course. They were both cases of injustice, one a particular one, the other a general one. The particular one was the case of a great difference being made in an English court between a woman of humble birth, and a woman of high birth. The other case, the general case, I had in mind to try to prevent England committing one of the greatest examples of injustice which have ever sullied her annals. I mean that all the males of the country should be endowed with the franchise, whilst not a single woman [?] was enfranchised, or if enfranchised was to be so endowed in a backstairs way. Such an injustice would be flagrant, and would be a slur not only on the women, but on the men, who would be insulted by the refusal to treat their mothers as free women. This could not be tolerated and I trust will be avoided. Then as to the act itself! Ever since the militant agitation began, it is the women who have suffered violence on their bodies as a result of their demand for justice. At first they submitted, but as the violence grew worse and worse they realized that it was... to submit to this violence, for the women are the gates of life to the nation, and it was therefore tantamount to murder to allow the violence to go on from worse to worse. Hence the women rather than submit to it, preferred to use violence to property in order to avoid it. They first damaged government property and you took no notice. They later damaged the property of the private citizen. But that could be repaired. And the [?] bodies of the women often could not be repaired. Three of my comrades have died for the violence inflicted on them on 18 November 1910. I read in the papers the other day that the soul and honor of a girl child of nine was valued in an English court of law at 30 pieces of silver. The reference is obvious to you. I felt that I must do damage that could not be repaired.

Now as to the form which my protest took. It has been misrepresented to you here. It was an open protest. On 8 December I dropped into the Fleet Street post office a packet of linen saturated in kerosene, having set it alight. I threw my matches in afterwards and was seen by a small boy. I proceeded down Fleet Street and went into a Lyons for lunch - now for three proofs that I did something. After ten minutes or a quarter of an hour, I heard several police whistles. They were not cab whistles, they were too long and many. On finishing lunch I walked down Fleet Street and came up by diverse ways into Fetter Lane. There I saw a plainclothes man giving instruction to a constable, it seemed to me about a pillar box nearby. As I came out of Fetter Lane facing the Fleet St post office, I saw two telegraph boys looking down the very aperture down which I had thrown my missive. Yet at first it was denied that anything was done. [In pencil above this line: 'Yet afterwards I was charged with this.'] As to the second case I determined to do two pillar boxes in the City which I accomplished. I then warned the Press that I would do one to be publicly taken, and did so. Otherwise nothing would have been known.

Now as to motive, it was purely political - [Here interrupted by Recorder to say that did not concern Jury]. Very well, I will keep to the question of guilt. Although technically you may find me guilty, morally I am not. The moral guilt lies upon you, the citizens of this country, who stand aside from the fight for the liberties of this country, and merely force the women to make protests how and where they may. We are... this country cannot possibly be genuinely democratic until the women, your mothers and sisters, stand side by side with you. Therefore the moral guilt lies upon you. I stand for the justice which you deny us. [This last sentence written in pencil.] In address to judges in mitigation of sentence, I pressed the question of political motive and said three things (a) to be allowed to pursue a vocation (b) not to be required to do prison tasks [?] and be able to keep... (c) to be allowed paper and letters, books. etc... Pointed out I would and write [?] book and asked to do so...

After I had finished, the old prosecutor began to read it through. He mumbled frightfully, so in a very loud voice I called to him to speak up. He looked sick and [ink stain] '...shout if you like!' All through this trial and other trials I had been struck by the shocking [triple underlining] acoustic properties of the Court, also by the way all the officials mumble from Sir Albert de Rutzen himself to the rest. Sometimes it seemed as if they did not mean the prisoner or public to hear, but this struck me as particularly unfair.

The old man mumbled on. When he came to the word 'decided' he apparently could not read his own writing and hesitated as to whether it was 'deceive' or what... In a very loud clear voice I told him it was 'decided' and spelt it to him 'd-e-c-i-d-e-d'. At this the court tittered and the gaoler beside me [stain obscures this next word]. At another point I pulled him up for turning [?] two sentences into one, saying... loudly, 'A full stop is wanted there, please...' The court was tickled. [This paragraph is stained all the way through the middle.]

By the way, when I made use of the expression 'incendiarism' in my statement, Sir Albert de Rutzen pulled me up, saying, 'One moment,' (then addressing Mr. Cooper) 'is it at your advice that the prisoner is speaking?' Mr. Cooper, obviously ill at ease, replied that he would rather answer that question in private. Then Sir Albert de Rutzen said, 'I understand that she is proceeding on her own idea,' and [of] Mr. Cooper that he [was] not able to prevent my speaking. [Lots crossed out in this paragraph and clearly words missing in her haste.]

That bold statement of mine no doubt decided Sir Albert de Rutzen. He announced that the case must go to the [court of] assizes.

MARTIN FIRRELL

The public artist Martin Firrell uses text in public space to promote debate. The more people think about, question and debate a topic, the more likely it becomes that change will occur.

Firrell uses language to engage directly with the public, promoting constructive dialogues, usually about marginalisation, equality and more equitable social organisation, with the aim of making the world more humane. His work has been summarised as 'art as debate'.

Socialart.work is a mass public art project created by Martin Firrell calling for greater social justice. It aims to create debate about power and its abuse, feminism, women's equality and gender, alternative forms of economic and social organisation, black power, counter-culture, and solidarity between people of different backgrounds and ethnicities.

The project includes posters, publications and events supported in 2018-19 by the digital media company Clear Channel UK.

Martin Firrell has been described in the Guardian as 'one of the capital's most influential public artists'.

More information about this project can be found at www.socialart.work. More information about the artist can be found at Wikipedia.

NOTES

NOTES

1. In May 1921, Ireland was partitioned under British law by the Government of Ireland Act, which created Northern Ireland. The Anglo-Irish Treaty signed on 6 December 1921 ended British rule in most of Ireland and, after a ten-month transitional period overseen by a provisional government, the Irish Free State was created as a self-governing Dominion on 6 December 1922. Northern Ireland remained within the United Kingdom.

2. The Suez Crisis was triggered by the invasion of Egypt in late 1956 by Israel, followed by the United Kingdom and France. The aims were to regain Western control of the Suez Canal and to remove Egyptian President Gamal Abdel Nasser who nationalised the canal. Political pressure from the United States, the Soviet Union and the United Nations eventually led to a withdrawal by the three invaders. The episode humiliated the United Kingdom and France and strengthened Nasser.

3. Perec 'Peter' Rachman (1919 - 29 November 1962) was a Polish-born landlord who operated in Notting Hill, London in the 1950s and early 1960s. He became notorious for his exploitation of his tenants, and the word 'Rachmanism' entered the Oxford English Dictionary as a synonym for the exploitation and intimidation of tenants.

4. Antonio Francesco Gramsci (22 January 1891 - 27 April 1937) was an Italian Marxist philosopher and communist politician. He differentiated between the traditional idea of an intelligentsia which regards itself as a class apart from society, and the thinking groups which every class produces from its own ranks organically. According to Gramsci, these 'organic intellectuals' are able to articulate the feelings and experiences that the masses cannot express for themselves.

5. The Black Power movement was prominent in the late 1960s and early 1970s, emphasising racial pride and the creation of black political and cultural institutions to nurture and promote black collective interests and advance black values. The term 'Black Power'

refers to a range of political goals, from defence against racial oppression, to the establishment of social institutions and a self-sufficient economy, including black-owned bookstores, cooperatives, farms, and media.

6. Mark Carlisle, Baron Carlisle of Bucklow, QC, DL, PC (7 July 1929 - 14 July 2005) was a Conservative British politician and MP for Runcorn from 1964 to 1983 and then for Warrington South until 1987. Created a life peer in November 1987, he served as Secretary of State for Education and Science from 1979 until 1981.

7. Alexander Ward Lyon (15 October 1931 - 30 September 1993) was a British Labour politician elected MP for the City of York in 1966. He was Minister of State at the Home Office, March 1974 - April 1976. He was a member of the Bar Council and of the Fabian Society. He was also a Methodist local preacher and secretary of the Leeds North West Constituency Labour Party. In 1981, he married Clare Short.

8. On 4 August 1972, Idi Amin, the President of Uganda declared that Britain would have to take responsibility for British subjects of Asian origin living in Uganda. A deadline was set of 8 November for British subjects to leave the country. At the time of the expulsion, there were approximately 80,000 people of South Asian descent in Uganda. 23,000 of these had had their applications for citizenship processed and accepted. Although they were ultimately exempted from the expulsion, many chose to leave voluntarily.

9. Lucas Industries plc was a Birmingham-based British manufacturer of motor industry and aerospace industry components. It was listed on the London Stock Exchange and was a FTSE 100 company.

10. Before the Suicide Act 1961, it was a crime to commit suicide, and anyone who attempted and failed could be prosecuted and imprisoned. The families of people who successfully committed suicide could also be prosecuted under certain circumstances.

NOTES

11. Sir Albert Bore (born 1946 in Ayrshire, Scotland) is a British nuclear physicist, academic and Labour Party politician. In 1981 he was selected to replace sitting MP John Sever as Labour parliamentary candidate in Birmingham Ladywood but parliamentary boundary changes before the 1983 General Election caused a new selection to be held, and Bore lost out to Clare Short.

12. Vera Joan Maynard (5 July 1921 - 27 March 1998) was an English Labour politician and trade unionist. She was a leading activist in the National Union of Agricultural Workers and joined the Labour Party in 1946. She was elected to Labour's National Executive Committee 1972 - 82 and 1983 - 87, and was Vice-Chair of the Labour Party 1980 - 81. She was elected in 1974 as MP for Sheffield Brightside and held the seat until she retired in 1987. She served on the Agriculture Select Committee 1975 - 87 and played a leading role in securing the passage of the Rent (Agriculture) Act 1976 which regulated the tied cottage system that had caused misery to rural workers.

13. Aneurin Bevan (15 November 1897 - 6 July 1960), often known as Nye Bevan, was a Welsh Labour Party politician and Minister for Health from 1945 to 1951. The son of a coal miner, Bevan was a lifelong champion of social justice, the rights of working people and democratic socialism. He was MP for Ebbw Vale, South Wales for 31 years. He was one of the chief spokesmen for the Labour Party's left wing, and of left-wing British thought in general. His single greatest accomplishment was the foundation of the National Health Service.

14. Rodney Kevan Bickerstaffe (6 April 1945 - 3 October 2017) was a popular trade union leader, calling for better rights and fairer treatment for staff working in public services. He was General Secretary of the National Union of Public Employees (1982 - 1993) and UNISON (1996 - 2001), Britain's largest trade union at the time.

15. The Prevention of Terrorism Acts were a series of Acts of Parliament from 1974 to 1989 that conferred emergency powers on police forces where they suspected terrorism. In 2000, the Acts were

NOTES

replaced with the more permanent Terrorism Act 2000, and the Prevention of Terrorism Act 2005.

16. Renée Short (née Gill, 26 April 1919 - 18 January 2003) was a British Labour Party politician. She was elected MP for Wolverhampton North East in 1964. She retained her seat at subsequent general elections until her retirement at the 1987 election. She also served on the Labour National Executive Committee 1970 - 81 and 1983 - 88. Short was an early advocate of abortion reform. She was for many years national president of the Campaign for Nursery Education, and of the Nursery Schools Association; and she was vice-president of the Women's National Cancer Control Campaign.

17. Neoliberalism is the 20th-century resurgence of 19th-century ideas associated with laissez-faire economic liberalism and free market capitalism. The term is associated with economic liberalisation policies such as privatisation, austerity, deregulation, free trade and reductions in government spending in order to increase the role of the private sector in the economy and society. These market-based ideas and the policies they inspired constitute a paradigm shift away from the post-war Keynesian consensus which lasted from 1945 to 1980.

18. Keynesian economics developed during and after the Great Depression from the ideas presented by John Maynard Keynes in his 1936 book, *The General Theory of Employment, Interest and Money*. Keynesian economists generally advocate a managed market economy - predominantly private sector, but with an active role for government intervention during recessions and depressions.

19. William Wilberforce (24 August 1759 - 29 July 1833) was a British politician, philanthropist, and a leader of the movement to abolish the slave trade. A native of Kingston upon Hull, Yorkshire, he began his political career in 1780, eventually becoming Member of Parliament for Yorkshire (1784 - 1812). He headed the parliamentary campaign against the British slave trade for twenty years until the

passage of the Slave Trade Act of 1807.

20. Shortly after her election in 1983, Clare Short implied the Government's Employment, Minister Alan Clark, was drunk at the despatch box. Clark's colleagues on the government benches in turn accused Short of using unparliamentary language and the Deputy Speaker, Ernest Armstrong, asked her to withdraw her accusation. Clark later admitted in his diaries that Short had been correct in her assessment.

21. The Birmingham pub bombings were carried out on 21 November 1974 when bombs exploded in two public houses in Birmingham, killing 21 people and injuring 182 others. Six Irishmen were sentenced to life imprisonment. The Birmingham Six, as they became known, maintained their innocence and insisted police had coerced them into signing false confessions. After 16 years in prison their convictions were declared unsafe and unsatisfactory, and quashed by the Court of Appeal in 1991. The episode is seen as one of the worst miscarriages of justice in British legal history.

22. Rudolf Joseph Lorenz Steiner (27 (or 25) February 1861 - 30 March 1925) was an Austrian philosopher, social reformer, architect, and esotericist. At the beginning of the 20th Century he founded the esoteric spiritual movement, anthroposophy, with roots in German idealist philosophy and theosophy. His approach to education aimed to awaken the 'physical, behavioural, emotional, cognitive, social, and spiritual' aspects of each individual, fostering creative and inquisitive thought.

23. The Angry Brigade was a far-left terrorist group responsible for a series of bomb attacks in England between 1970 and 1972. The group used small bombs to maximise media exposure for their demands while keeping collateral damage to a minimum. Jake Prescott was arrested in 1971 and sentenced to 15 years imprisonment. In February 2002, Prescott apologised for his role in bombing the house of Conservative politician, Robert Carr, and called on other members of the Angry Brigade to also come forward.

NOTES

24. Leonard Robert Carr, Baron Carr of Hadley, PC (11 November 1916 - 17 February 2012) was a Conservative Party politician. He served as Secretary of State for Employment and was responsible for the Industrial Relations Act 1971. In 1972, he was appointed Home Secretary after the resignation of Reginald Maudling.

25. The Red Army Faction (RAF, German: Rote Armee Fraktion), also known as the Baader-Meinhof Gang, was a West German far-left militant organisation founded in 1970. Key early figures included Andreas Baader, Gudrun Ensslin, Horst Mahler and Ulrike Meinhof. Ulrike Meinhof was involved in Baader's escape from gaol in 1970. The West German government as well as most Western media considered the Red Army Faction to be a terrorist organisation.

26. Terence James MacSwiney (28 March 1879 - 25 October 1920) was an Irish playwright, author and politician. He was elected as Sinn Féin Lord Mayor of Cork during the Irish War of Independence in 1920. He was arrested by the British government on charges of sedition and imprisoned in Brixton Prison. His death there in October 1920, after 74 days on hunger strike, brought him and the Irish Republican campaign to international attention.

27. Chartism was a working-class movement for political reform in Britain. The movement existed from 1838 to 1857 taking its name from the People's Charter of 1838. The Chartists used petitions, signed by millions of working people, and mass meetings to pressure Parliament to enfranchise all men.

28. On 1 August 1915, the Irish revolutionary, Patrick Pearse, gave a graveside oration at the funeral of Jeremiah O'Donovan Rossa, a prominent member of the Irish Republican Brotherhood. The oration concluded: 'They think that they have pacified Ireland. They think that they have purchased half of us and intimidated the other half. They think that they have foreseen everything, think that they have provided against everything; but the fools, the fools, the fools! - they have left us our Fenian dead, and while Ireland holds these graves, Ireland unfree shall never be at peace.' The oration roused

Irish republican feeling and was a significant element in the lead-up to the Easter Rising of 1916.

29. Robert Gerard Sands (9 March 1954 - 5 May 1981) was a member of the IRA who died on hunger strike while an inmate at Maze Prison. The 1981 hunger strike was a protest against the removal of Special Category Status. During the strike, Sands was elected to the British Parliament as an Anti H-Block candidate.

30. Estelle Sylvia Pankhurst (5 May 1882 - 27 September 1960) was an English campaigner for the suffragette movement, a prominent Left Communist and later an activist in the cause of anti-fascism. She spent much of her later life agitating on behalf of Ethiopia, where she eventually moved. Her son, Richard Keir Pethick Pankhurst OBE (3 December 1927 - 16 February 2017) was a British academic, founding member of the Institute of Ethiopian Studies, and former professor at the University of Addis Ababa in Ethiopia.

31. The Factory Acts were a series of UK labour laws to regulate the conditions of industrial employment. The early Acts concentrated on regulating the hours of work and moral welfare of young children employed in cotton mills but were effectively unenforced until the Act of 1833 established a professional Factory Inspectorate. A strong humanitarian campaign was championed by Anthony Ashley-Cooper (later the 7th Earl of Shaftesbury). Ashley-Cooper led the 'Ten-Hour Movement' aiming to reduce the working day for children under sixteen.

www.ingramcontent.com/pod-product-compliance
Lightning Source LLC
Chambersburg PA
CBHW020258030426
42336CB00010B/817